COWGIRLS
Don't Cry

VETERINARIAN
RANCHER
BAR ROOM DANCER

MARINEL J. POPPIE DVM

This book is dedicated to Hai Karatie[+], faithful
friend for 36 years.

Hai Karatie[+], photo by Carolie Addison

TABLE OF CONTENTS

Me, Marinel, 1 year old.

1

CHILD OF THE BIG SKY

Snow-capped Rocky Mountains cradled the lush fertile valley the Indians called "Valley of the Flowers." Lodge pole pine grew up to the timberline, shading the remaining winter snow. Quaking aspen leaves shimmered and danced in the summer breeze. Three large rivers wound through the vast valley, converging into the mighty Missouri River. Moose, elk, deer, bear, antelope, mountain lion, mountain sheep, mountain goats and mountain men thrived in this wild and beautiful land.

Early one morning in July 1940, I appeared on the scene. Lucky to be born on this day, in this beautiful valley, I too was enveloped in the cradle of the Rocky Mountains and in the arms of my Montana family and heritage.

My Montana roots were deep and loyal. Father was a tall and handsome attorney who wore many hats. He looked like a combination of Jimmy Stewart and Dean Martin, and could

Dad

Dad and Ship

have fit in well with the Rat Pack. He also excelled as a rancher, hunter and gold miner. Considered the best-dressed attorney in the area, at the ranch is where he was happiest in his worn Levi's and dirty western hat. Mom was pretty in a fine porcelain sort of way, well educated, socially correct and a proper mother. She was a direct descendant of John Marshall, Chief Justice of the U.S. Supreme Court, and his first cousin, Thomas Jefferson.

Father's side of the family homesteaded this land in the 1800s. Granddad established his first law office in Butte, Montana in 1898 where he became assistant city attorney, later to move to Bozeman where for 47 years he was prominent in legal, civic and fraternal affairs.

In 1947, Montana's Governor, Sam Stewart, appointed Granddad as the first judge of the eighteens judicial circuit. Father was born in 1909, not long after the Indian Wars had subsided and, until his last day, delighted in telling me he was going to give me back to the Indians! Dad began his law practice with his father. Later he was elected county attorney and served the Bozeman law profession as an attorney for sixty-five years.

Bozeman, the western town we called home, was not too large, about five thousand. My grandmother's brother, Walter Hartman, drafted the bill that established Montana State University. He was a prominent attorney and judge for forty-eight years. Granny's other brother Charles Hartman was

Brother Bud

a district judge, member of congress for six years and U.S. ambassador to Ecuador. Granny and Granddad lived with us at first. Granny was smart, sweet and gentle, and national president of the Rebekah Lodge. She only wore dresses—pants were for men—but she was a good ranch hand when needed. Brother Bud was three years older than me, and my constant companion. Bud and I were both short like Granddad and had big blue eyes

Earliest memories are sorted. Warm, fresh cookies from the neighbor ladies, beautiful colors that danced through the leaded glass in the bay window of our old-fashioned, two-story house, Granny's purple violets and Granddad stoking the coal furnace in the basement where Granny made lye soap, our big garden where I collected bugs, the smells of lilacs and sweet peas, the cabbage barrel for winter storage, the root cellar, chicken coop and the barn all imprinted on my being.

A severe fungal infection in the ear kept my father from World War II overseas action. But, as a lieutenant and attorney in the Navy, he hand delivered classified information to the first United Nations conference in San Francisco, where world leaders including Winston Churchill and Joseph Stalin gathered. We traveled by train with Dad to his various assignments. I loved trains! Dad would carry me up and down the aisle on his shoulders. Sailors would sing to me and pass me back and forth in the rocking car. I learned to sing:

"Bell bottom trousers,
Coat of navy blue.
I love my sailor boy
And he loves me too"

Sometimes we couldn't go with Dad and stayed at the naval base in San Francisco. I knew Mom was lonely so I would go next door to the park to find her a sailor. Singing my sailor song to them, and holding their hands, they gladly followed me home to meet my mom. Why wouldn't she invite them into the house? I wanted to show them my room and my bug collection! Never having been told there were bad people in the world, I happily lived in a world of no fear. Mom spoiled that for me. She told me a little girl had been abducted in a park, killed and dumped in the ocean, and she abruptly stopped me from bringing any more sailors home.

I got my first black eye in San Francisco. Some neighbor kids repeatedly threw their kitten out the second-story window to watch it land on its feet. This broke my heart. I got punched in the eye and my clothes ripped to shreds when I tried to save the kitten.

In New York City, Dad held my hand as we walked down the street. I looked up at the tall buildings, as high as I could, but still could not see the sky. When we got home to Montana, I asked him who cut the tops off of all our buildings.

When I was five, Granny and Granddad moved out of the house we all shared in town and they built a log home in the country. The large acreage had a beautiful creek that wound through the pasture. Its crystal-blue water sparkled like diamonds as it raced over rocks, looking for a place to settle in deep green pools full of fish, frogs, snakes, water bugs and dragonflies.

Bud and me with hired hand.

Our first car

On warm summer days, Bud and I waded and swam there. The water was sweet and pure to drink. The banks of the stream were lined with sweet timothy hay and masses of wildflowers.

There were so many bugs to find in the water, hay and flowers. Granny saved all of her glass jars for my insect collections. With a nail and hammer, I pounded out air holes in the lids, added grass, leaves and a little water so my bugs would be happy. When they died, it would be so sad, so I made a cemetery near Granny's house where all my little friends were carefully buried. I made each one a cross out of sticks and baling twine, then singing a prayer I had learned at Sunday School, I buried them.

Our family had survived the Great Depression by selling the cattle ranch and buying a sheep ranch. Going to the ranch with Dad and Granddad in the Model T was better than a carnival ride. Fuel was still being rationed, so Granddad would turn off the motor and we'd coast down the long hills to the bottom. The men would then get out, turn a crank in the front of the car and off we would go, up and down over the rolling dirt road with the wind in our hair, singing old Western tunes. Thousands of sheep, with brands painted on their backs, grazed the rolling hills below the mountains. Dad said: "These sheep are guarded by good Irish sheepherders and their sheep dogs. You never pay a sheepherder until the end of lambing season or they'll go to town, get drunk and leave the sheep to the wolves!"

As a five-year-old, I helped Dad snare gophers. He'd make a long snare with baling twine and place a loop around the gopher hole. We'd lie on our stomachs and wait and wait. When the gopher emerged from its hole, Dad would jerk the line and fling the poor little ball of fur through the air. I think Dad thought it was like fly fishing for trout. Our dogs would then tear into the little animal and quickly kill it. I didn't want Dad to see me cry, but it nearly broke my heart. I decided then and there that when I got back to Granddad's farm, I would snare my own gophers, put them in a nice, big jar, feed them oats and keep them for pets. By the end of summer, I had a lot of pet gophers, all with special names.

Sometimes Bud would help me snare. One day, when we had set our snare, we caught the wildest creature. It leaped through the air like no gopher we'd ever seen. "Sister, I think we've got a bobcat," Bud said. Then that wild, furry, fighting thing bit the baling twine in half and two weasels ran off!

We would catch frogs and snakes too. Bud liked to help me catch garter snakes. We'd wrap them around our necks and arms like Tarzan, but Granny wouldn't let us take them home.

One warm, sunny day, I found some frogs under a bridge. Bud, who was seven and had his .22-gauge rifle and was hunting for gophers in a nearby pasture. An old truck came down the gravel road and stopped above the

Bud, (12 years old) his gun and Clancy

bridge. A man with a straw hat got out and climbed down the bank. "What are you doing, little girl?" he asked. "Catching frogs," I replied. "Do you want to help me?" Wading into the creek, he picked me up and swung me in the air, hitting my head on the bridge bottom. He then swung me into the creek. I thought this was a strange man and remembered the little girl who was abducted in San Francisco. I got scared but didn't want him to know, so I asked him over and over to please put me down so I could catch my frogs. He just laughed and kept swinging me. Bud came to see if I had any snakes. As he slid down the bank with his rifle, the man dropped me into the water, ran up the bank, jumped in his truck throwing gravel every which way as he sped off. When I told Dad, who was County Attorney at the time, about the man who played too rough, he was more upset than I'd ever seen him. Sheriff Don came to our house and he and Dad questioned me. "What did he look like? What color was his truck?" I could only tell them he wore a straw hat and didn't like frogs much! A statewide manhunt was launched but the man in the straw hat was never found.

Bud and I spent most of time together, especially at Granddad's farm. Granddad had a steer we named Jug Head, we would climb on him and make him go by poking his fresh brand. Racing across the pasture, we usually fell off. Sometimes we fell just because we giggled so hard. Often barefoot, we would make footprints in fresh cow pies. After a week of drying, we'd retrieve them on a wooden board, paint them and proudly give them to our mother, just like Bud had learned to do with plaster of Paris in his art class at school.

One evening we were out by the cottonwood trees, they were big with many branches and in the summertime, their white, fluffy seeds would cover the ground like new-fallen snow. Suddenly, a big Hereford bull charged us! Trees were no strangers to us. We were sure Tarzan was our next-of-kin and we climbed to safety. The bull was serious and violently butted the tree for a long, long time. We climbed higher and snuggled together in the fork of the tree. It was getting dark. Finally Granddad came home from work and saw our predicament. He drove across the pasture to our rescue, but the big bull turned on him and rammed his car. After several minutes of honking the horn and driving in circles, the bull tired, lost interest and ambled away.

Granddad had saved our lives! Granddad smiled at me with soft gentle eyes. He taught me to play cribbage and we made a cribbage board out of an elk antler. When we went to town, he always took me to eat pickled pigs feet. Granddad was judge for several years after that, but suddenly died from a heart attack when Bud and I were still young. I didn't understand. Bud and I were not included at the funeral. Our family protected us from the reality of the loss. I only knew Granddad was gone and every one seemed sad. No one we knew had ever died before.

Bud and I spent a lot of time tricking each other. There were beehives across the road from Granddad's farm. Bud asked me to help him find snakes in that pasture. He told me the hives were sheep graves and that, if I loved animals, I should pick some wildflowers and put them on the graves. The bee-keeper had built a high fence around his hives to keep cattle out, but I scaled the fence with my freshly picked flowers singing a little Sunday school prayer as I placed flowers on the graves. I wasn't afraid of bees. At home, I could catch them in the hollyhocks with my bare hands. Suddenly, there were a lot of bees and I was being stung! I could hear Bud laughing and realized I'd been tricked. Dropping my flowers, I climbed back over the fence as fast as I could with the bees still following me. I grabbed Bud. We ran all the way home. I was so mad at being tricked, but it was nice to know that Bud got stung too. Granny put pink calamine lotion on my stings and Bud was sent to bed.

Granddad owned a couple of horses. One was an old, black mare I named Black Beauty, the other a young, unbroken bay gelding. The bay was somewhat gentle, but not broke to ride. Dad came out to the farm to show his friend the horse and asked me if I wanted to sit on it while they talked business. His friend held the halter rope as Dad lifted me on the geldings' back. The horse reared and bolted. The friend hung on as best he could. I barely stayed on by grabbing a big chunk of mane. The horse settled down and Dad pulled me off, but I saw blood pouring from his friend's hand. He'd wrapped the rope around his hand and, when the horse bolted, four of his fingers were pulled off. Dad rushed him, and what we could find of his fingers, to the hospital. The surgery was unsuccessful; the man was disfigured for life.

Bud and me driving Black Beauty.

After hanging on to that gelding, I was certain I could ride any horse by myself. Dad said "not yet sister" but took me to all the nearby rodeos and Wild West shows. Mom and Dad bought me the perfect outfit: a red-fringed skirt with matching red cowgirl hat and real red cowboy boots that I proudly wore. The shows were thrilling: Trick horses, trick riders hanging upside down from their horses as they raced around the arena and, best of all, Roman riders who stood up with one foot on each of a matched-pair of glistening horses that jumped through hoops of fire. I loved the bucking horses and the bull riding. In 1949, Casey Tibbs "the Rainbow Rider" and World Champion Cowboy, entered our rodeo. He could ride any bucking horse or bull, his purple chaps fanning the air. I was sure I could ride just like Casey, having stayed on Granddad's bay and Jug Head the steer! All-Around World Champion Cowboys Benny Reynolds and Jim Shoulders competed in our rodeos a few years later.

Dad said I was too little to have my own horse, but I made do. Our two-story house in town had a parlor where the men would retire after dinner to smoke cigars and drink whiskey. Mom, Granny and I were not allowed in that room during parlor time. In the parlor was a big wooden rocking chair with arms and an old record player. We had old classic Western records and this was my special place during the day. Wearing my red cowgirl outfit, I'd turn on the records, climb up on the arm of the rocking chair and spend hours singing along with Gene Autry, Roy Rogers and my other favorite cowboys. Tying a rope on the arm of the rocker, I would hold these reins and dream I was riding my horse across the hay meadow.

Bud and I were given an allowance of 20 cents a week for working around the house and garden. Every Saturday we'd walk to the Ellen Theater and pay 12 cents to see a movie on the big screen. Roy Rogers, Gene Autry, Hop Along Cassidy and Tarzan were our favorites. I always wore my red cowgirl outfit and now had a cap gun with a holster. Bud also brought his cap gun. We had to empty the caps from our guns before they let us into the theater, but this didn't slow us down. We'd spend the next two hours firing away at the bad guys and singing along with our heroes. Tarzan wasn't a cowboy, but he was still our hero. We loved to watch him swing through the trees, catch the bad guys in the quicksand and build hidden traps in the jungle! When the movie "The Red Shoes" came to town, Mom made us go to get some culture. We hated it. We hid under the seats and screamed until the manager escorted us out!

After the movies we'd buy a nickel Spud-nut then go to the trick store. Pooling the rest of our money, we'd buy whatever gadget we could afford and plan our strategies for tricking and scaring the neighbor kids. We accumulated a good collection of masks, rubber knives, ropes, swords, balloons, magic paint and mild trick explosives. New Year's Eve we decided to trick Dad. Having to stay home with the baby sitter, we got a pack of Dad's cigarettes, carefully loaded it with little sticks of explosives and placed it back on the night-stand. Morning found us waiting outside our parents' bedroom, lying on the hallway floor, peeking under the crack below the door. We thought they'd never wake up. Suddenly, we heard the explosion we'd been waiting for—Boom, followed by words we'd never heard before! The door flew open and there stood Dad in his shorts, his eyebrows on fire and black soot across his face. We had never crossed Dad before and never seen him so startled and mad. We flew down the stairs, and hid in an old building in the alley until after dark. Cold and hunger finally sent us home. Dad appeared, minus most of his eyebrows. He didn't hit us, but he didn't have to. We were punished in other ways and sent to our rooms without our comics.

Birch trees in front of our first house

Although Bud and I were the littlest kids on the block, we were the fastest runners, best tree climbers and very best tricksters. I'm not sure why we delighted so much in tricking our friends. I think we got the mindset from Abbott & Costello or Laurel & Hardy movies, and definitely from Tarzan. Comic books also gave us information. My favorite was Plastic Man. Our house was perfect for playing tricks. It had an attic, lots of closets and a laundry chute from the second floor to the coal room. There was a cool and creepy basement, a banister along the stairs, a cabbage barrel buried in the garden, a root cellar, a chicken house, a barn and, best of all, two huge birch trees in the front yard. I had a witch's costume and delighted in climbing the birch trees as a witch. Certain I could fly, I swung through the branches like Tarzan. The trees provided the perfect setting to drop water balloons on people as they walked along the sidewalk. We also had a maze of ropes throughout the trees that were great for hauling up props like our fluorescent life-sized skeleton, our ghost, boxes of balloons, water, fireworks, old rotten vegetables and many more treasures.

I had a boy friend named Prunie. He had no teeth as he had bitten the electrical cord while his mother was vacuuming, but he was my good friend and a good tree climber. Sometimes Mother would let me have a sleepover with a girlfriend. I asked her if Prunie could come sleepover too. She said "No." This puzzled me, as I liked Prunie. Mother said only married girls could sleep with boys. So I asked Prunie if he'd marry me up in the birch tree. He said yes and I made a beautiful white wedding dress out of Granny's best lace tablecloth. Prunie wore his dress shirt and Bud married us in the tree. That night Prunie came over with his latest comic books and told Mom we were married now and he was there for our sleepover. Dad took him home and shook his head at me as he tucked me into bed. I was given no explanation. I was just tucked in with my large collection of stuffed animals. No dolls, Bud said those were sissy, girl things!

A friend told me Prunie had killed a bird. I was sad and mad. I had a cemetery for animals, not only at Granddad's farm, but also in back of the garden at the house in town. I laid plans to teach Prunie never to kill a bird again. I would make a Tarzan trap! The wooden top of the steel-rimmed, 50-gallon cabbage barrel buried at the back of the garden came off easily. I carefully laid corn stalks over the hole and my Tarzan trap was ready. When Prunie came over to play, I told him I was mad, but would forgive him if he'd bring his little dead bird over and help me bury it in my cemetery. Soon he returned with the dead robin. Holding his hand, I carefully led him toward my Tarzan trap. Suddenly Prunie and the Robin fell through the corn stalks and into the barrel! I tried to see them but they were covered with corn stalks. After awhile, I yelled for him to come out but got no response. I got scared and ran to the upstairs window where I could see the garden. It seemed like hours before I saw the corn stalks move. A bloody hand reached up to the metal rim. Then I saw Prunies' head emerge. His face was so bloody that he looked like a monster! I locked the bedroom door and hid under the bed. Two days later he came over with multiple stitches in his lip and nose. The metal rim had sliced his upper lip and nose from his face. "I know it was an accident," he said. "Did you find the dead robin for your cemetery?"

I collected horse statues. I was so proud of them and carefully displayed them in my room. Our house cleaner, Erma, didn't like our dog so Bud and I didn't like her. The days she came to clean, we stayed outside. Because she tormented our hunting dog, we'd torment her by ringing the doorbell and hiding in the bushes. Apparently Erma was a little unstable. One day she lost it. She took the broom to my room and knocked down all my beautiful horse statues. Nearly all of them broke. Dad decided Erma would have to go. As county attorney, he knew her brother had cut off another brother's head off with an axe. Because Erma might be genetically unstable, he considered Bud and me likely candidates to push her over the edge. Several years later, I was walking that same dog down Main Street. Erma passed us. Our dog had not forgotten his tormentor and lunged for her. He'd never been vicious before. This convinced me that animals seldom recover from being abused.

Our neighbor girl was afraid of balloons. Bud and I knew Dad had a real sword from the Navy, or somewhere. We invited Katy to come to Bud's room to read comics. We had filled his closet with balloons. When we told her to get her comic book out of the closet, we closed the door on her. Sticking the sword through a crack in the door, we began to pop balloons. Poor Katy was terrified. When she was let out, she came at us with a vengeance. To escape, we jumped in the laundry chute and landed safely in the basement.

The rodeo was coming to town. I begged Dad to let me ride a horse in the parade. Finally he said I could ride Black Beauty, Granddad's old, black work-horse. Dad also said I'd better wear jeans, not my red cowgirl skirt. Black Beauty was fat and slow. Dad and Uncle Pete saddled her up

Riding Black Beauty, November, 1949

and put me aboard. I could not begin to reach the long stirrups but didn't
care. Dad and Uncle Pete slowly followed me five miles to town where they
had arranged for a friend to ride with me. I was the proudest rider in the
parade. I waved at everyone as the bands played and old Black Beauty slowly
ambled along. Dad even said I could keep Black Beauty at the house in town
that night. I rode her all day, taking her across all the neighbors' yards. As I
couldn't get on the big mare without help, I found a long stick to knock on
their doors so they would come outside and see me on my beautiful horse.
That was one of my grandest days and I knew that some day, I'd have my own
horse to ride.

I finally got to go to school. I loved art, music and P.E. I thought all but
one boy was a sissy and fought with them all the time. Mom could not
believe that I'd come home minus several buttons and with torn and dirty
clothes nearly every day. Girls had to wear dresses unless it was wintertime
and freezing cold. I hated dresses and, to rub it in, Bud and Dad called me
"Skirts." I got my first crush on a boy when I was in fourth-grade. He was
the one who wasn't a sissy. I couldn't beat him up. He hit me in the chin by
accident splitting it so wide open that it required several stitches. I decided
he was special. I even wrote a song about him:

> *"Vote for Howie, vote for Howie.*
> *He's the sweetest boy on earth.*
> *Vote for Howie, Vote for Howie*
> *He's in my heart for ever worth."*

Little did I know that when I became a senior in high school, we would
be engaged!

Winter snows were deep. Walking home from fourth grade, I spotted a
steep shed roof in the back alley. It had a beautiful crown of soft, white snow.
Climbing to the top from the other side, I jumped and landed in the deep
snowdrift that had come off the roof like an avalanche. It was so fun! I knew
I'd have a soft landing. The snow was three-feet deep in town that year. I
wanted to make a snow angel before I left, but couldn't pull my legs out of
the heavy snow. I was stuck. It was getting dark and there was no one around
to help. I was getting very cold, as I only had my school clothes on. When I

Dad on horseback

didn't come home by dark, neighbors were called to help look for me. They knew I liked to walk home up the alley. After a couple of hours, a neighbor found me and pulled me out. I learned an early lesson about avalanches and, in later years, always respected avalanche signs on the ski hill.

I loved the snow and cold winters. Mom used to make vanilla snow cones for my friends and me. I remember finding yellow snow out in our yard. I used the snow to make snow cones for my friends too. They paid a penny a cone. It wasn't until sometime later Mom realized what I was doing. She explained the yellow snow I found in the yard was not made of vanilla! I was told I had to close shop.

Dad built a log cabin in the mountains. It was the last building up the canyon, and only a mile from a ski hill. They had night skiing there! Bud and I would ski across the frozen creek to the hill. It had a rope tow and good runs. I loved to night ski when it was snowing. The big, soft flakes drifting down past the lights looked magical. Even after we would go back to the cabin, I would stay outside, snug in the deep snow, watching the beauty of the falling flakes. I could see my family inside, around the big, fireplace, but

I preferred to stay outside until they called me in for bed. I had a little feather bed on the floor and a big, black bear rug next to me. On the walls hung mounted heads of moose, deer and elk. They all had cigarettes hanging out of their mouths. I thought they were so magnificent and decided when I got my own horse and, if it ever died, I'd have it stuffed, thus keeping it forever.

Our cabin was more than a mile from any plowed road in the winter. We all had snowshoes and our big dog, Clancy, would pull the toboggan with our groceries to the cabin. We cooked our meals in the beautiful sunken fireplace Dad had built and melted snow for drinking water.

Mom didn't like our old-fashioned house in town, but I loved it. She wanted Dad to buy a modern house on the other side of town. I couldn't imagine leaving my birch trees and the chicken coop Dad had said Bud and I could use for a clubhouse. We had painted all the walls different colors. We had an old Victrola record player and a couple of old chairs. It was our secret hideaway: only our best friends could enter, and only if they knew the password.

There was one boy in my class who fought with me all the time. Deciding it was time for him to learn not to hit me, I laid a plan to teach him a lesson. I told Ned if he wanted to be my friend, he should pick me up and walk me to school. I told him I would be waiting in the clubhouse. We he arrived, I invited him in to look at the record player, then I ran out and locked him inside before going to school. Ned never got to school. The teacher called his home and the police began a search. My lips were sealed. After school, I went back to the chicken coop. Ned was still there, screaming and pounding on the door. The thought of leaving him all night was tempting, but I knew I'd be in even bigger trouble. So I said, "Why don't you crawl out the hole where the other chickens go out." That made Ned even madder! He was big and I didn't think he could fit through the chicken door. I could hear him grunting and yelling as he tried to squeeze out. Suddenly, he was free. I started running home but he tackled me, rubbed my face in the dirt, stuffed my mouth with old leaves, tore my coat and pulled my hair. I tried to reach my room without my parents seeing me, but couldn't. Mom said I'd have to buy my own clothes if I did not stop fighting with the boys. Dad just grinned.

Bud and I did most everything together. I'm sure he wanted to ditch me, but I went where he went. When our folks went out at night, they would hire a babysitter. We'd fight like crazy. Bud would hit me over the head with various objects until my head split open. He always hit me from the front. I'd sneak up on him and crack his head a good one from the back. Nothing bleeds better than head wounds! The babysitter would freak out and call our parents to come home. Our proudest moments were in the doctor's office, getting our stitches. We never cried; we carried our battle wounds with great pride. To this day, I can see scars on my

Our Montana family picnic with a bear

forehead. Buds' were to the back of his head. That Christmas Dad gave us each a set of regulation boxing gloves and some boxing lessons.

Dad bought a surplus Army ambulance from World War II. It was brown with a big red cross on each side and it had numerous bullet holes. We hung four hammocks in the back, and named the ambulance George. It could cover any rough terrain, making it perfect for camping trips. We may have created the original off-road camper. Dad was a wild driver—the steeper the mountains, the better. To keep from tipping over on those steep slopes, we'd all have to stand on the upside running board. Once, mom got so scared she bailed out saying, "I would rather be eaten by a bear than ride with your Dad." After she got out, Dad just drove on. There were a lot of bears and moose where we went. I jumped out and ran back to save Mom who was sitting on a log, crying. Was she glad to see me! Hiking for miles, we caught up to the ambulance, Dad was fishing.

Mom had a lot of bridge parties at our house. She gave me a whistle that looked like a bird. When you blew on its tail, it chirped. During one bridge party, I ran around blowing on that whistle. Apparently I inhaled it, as I chirped with each breath I took! I remember getting dizzy. Mom said I turned blue. The bridge party ladies picked me up by my heels and bounced me upside down until the whistle dislodged from my trachea, and I could breathe again. Poor Mom, I'm sure she wanted a quiet little girl who'd love to wear dresses and serve cookies to her guests.

Moving to a modern house remained my mother's dream. I could hear the fights between my father and her. She finally won. We were told we'd be moving to the other side of town. Mom advertised my little brass bed for sale and told me some one was coming to look at it. I loved my bed. I couldn't lose it. Patiently, I unscrewed all the hardware that held it together. A large lady in a straw hat arrived to look at it. "It's lovely" she said. As she sat down on my bed, it fell apart and she rolled across my room. The sale was off. I saved my bed!

Montana's warm summer days were full of excitement. I had a weekly schedule. On Tuesdays, Bud and I would go to the courthouse to see Dad, who was county attorney, and Granddad, who was the judge. Their secretaries treated us like we were special and gave us candy. I will always remember the strong smell of cigars. We were allowed to visit the jail and considered ourselves friends with the sheriff and his deputies. They'd let us visit the prisoners. Some " jail birds" were nice, but some were scary. A prisoner was sleeping with his foot hanging out between the cell's bars. Bud dared me to bite his toe. I didn't want to be called a "sissy," so I took the dare. He let out a blood-curling scream! We ran out side as fast as we could as the sheriff looked at us in disbelief.

On Wednesdays, my girlfriend and I went to her father's funeral parlor. She knew her way around as we went room to room. The basement had scary instruments. The caskets were open. She said dead people liked us to visit them and we should shake their hands. There was this big man with a long, white beard in a golden casket. I shook his big hand. My friend yelled for me to run, that her dad was coming. I dropped his hand over the side of the casket and ran in to the alley. I told my friend the big man was Santa Claus and I shouldn't have run away from him.

On Thursdays, Bud and I would walk five miles out of town to the livestock sale yard and slaughter-house. We'd watch as the cows and horses were sold, and then watch as the cows were butchered. One crazy guy named

Jake stomped the guts with his big, rubber boots to make fertilizer and feed. He scared me. I was so sad to see the cows killed, I'd cry all the way home, but would show up again every Thursday. I wanted to save those cows and made plans for their rescue. One Thursday, I got Bud to go play with his friends and I went to the slaughterhouse alone. The corrals behind the big building were full of cows and the gates weren't locked. I snuck from corral to corral, opening the gates to free the cows. By the time Jake and the other slaughterhouse guys showed up, cows were running everywhere. The more the men yelled, the faster the cattle ran. They ran up the hills and into the timber. I hid behind the tall reeds in a nearby pond, feeling like Tarzan, having saved the animals. I didn't leave my hiding place until nearly dark. When I got home, there was talk on the radio about cows running free from the sale yard.

Sweet William was my pet skunk. He'd been de-scented. I often took him downtown on a leash. One day he disappeared and the whole neighborhood looked for him. One neighbor, Elmer, was fishing and thought he'd found him. Elmer threw dirt clods at the skunk to be sure he was Sweet William. The skunk seemed to be safe, so he crossed the creek on a log and picked him up. It was not Sweet William and the skunk let go with both barrels!

Bozeman Girl Has Skunk--Deodorized--For Pet

Bozeman residents have no reason to run for cover when they [see] [Mari]nel Bolinger, daughter [of Mr.] and Mrs. H. A. Bolinger, [with] her new pet, "Sweet Wil-[liam"] has been showing [William] around Bozeman's business district on a leash [for a] few days to the amusement [of] tourists and local residents alike, who, according to [Marinel,] "always want to pet him [when] they find out 'Willie' has [been] deodorized."

"Willie," as Marinel affectionately calls her newest pet, is one [of five] young skunks (Marinel says he is "about two months [old]) caught by Tom Sabo, 14-year-old son of Dr. and Mrs. F. [Sa]bo, on Dr. H. G. Klemme's [ranch] south of Bozeman. One [of the] two are in Billings and two [are in] Bozeman, the other belonging [to] Ken Sullivan who, according to [Mari]nel, who with "a friend" seems [to] be doing a good business on [the] "skunk market."

"I'm teaching Willie some [tri]cks, just like a dog," Marinel says. "He can be bashful and [hi]de his face when I tell him to," [and] next I'm going to try to [te]ach him how to sit up and roll over."

Marinel, who celebrated her tenth birthday recently, also said she had two other pets—a horned toad, which her brother brought her from the national Scout Jamboree, and a "big, brown dog named Clancy that was mean to Willie at first but sticks up for him now."

She didn't seem too worried about Willie defending himself though, as she told how Willie could bite and showed one mark on her hand to prove it.

Those who know Marinel weren't surprised when she got Willie for a pet. As Garvin Wyman, who operates the West Babcock grocery, says "you never know what she's liable to turn up with next so I wasn't a bit surprised when she came over for some groceries and walked in with a skunk."

Her latest pets, anyway they were yesterday, are some polliwogs.

When asked how she happened to get a skunk for a pet, Marinel replied quickly that she "could have Willie or a bike and a party, so she took Willie.

"But," she said confidently, "I think I'll get the bike anyway."

Article from the Bozeman Daily Chronicle, August 5th, 1950

Poor Elmer, he was a mess and had to burn his clothes. Sweet William was never found and, after that, nobody else wanted to look for him.

As summer shadows lengthened, the vegetables in the garden were ready to eat or can for the long winter that would soon arrive. Bud and I were allowed to sell vegetables to our neighbors. We loaded our red wagon, selling them door-to-door, we made enough money to buy some Charlie Russell Western prints. After our garden had been harvested, I gathered the remaining vegetables from our neighbor's gardens and put them in my red wagon to sell up and down the block. Driving home from work, Dad saw me with my wagon full of vegetables. Putting on his brakes, he backed up and asked me where I'd gotten them. I had to tell the truth. He told me to go to each house, apologize and return the vegetables as well as the money. Humiliated and embarrassed, I learned a life-long lesson.

Winter was coming. The warm summer days turned short and cold. Cedar waxwings ate the red berries in the yard, got intoxicated and flew into the windows. Flocks of Canada geese and mallard ducks filled the sky, honking as they flew in their V formations. The leaves fell, covering the ground in a canvas of red and golden colors. The cabbage barrel was filled and the storm windows installed. Coal for the furnace and wood for the fireplace were brought in. Finally, the soft snow began to fall and we were enveloped in white. The skating rinks would open soon. My first skates were two-runners, but I soon graduated to single blades. I loved my new high-laced, white skates with their one shiny, sharp blade! At first I had to wear Bud's old skating clothes, but eventually got a white fur coat, hat and a muff to warm my hands. My long, red wool scarf flowed behind me as music played and I whirled around the ice.

While walking home from the skating rink, we'd eat snow and icicles. Bud dared me to lick the guide wire that came down from the power pole. I couldn't refuse a dare, so I did what he said. My tongue stuck to the pole as soon as I licked it. It hurt so much, but I couldn't yell. My tears turned into long icicles. I thought I'd die there. Bud ran home and told Dad who raced to my rescue with a large container of hot water. He slowly poured the water over my tongue and the metal until I finally came free. My mouth hurt for days and I couldn't speak. I had no desire to speak to my brother!

I was to start fifth-grade when we moved to our new house. I was still the smallest kid in class. At least now I weighed more than forty pounds. I think I topped the scale around sixty pounds, but I was a fast runner and won the softball throw. Our new house was nice even though mom had it painted pink. We had the only pink house in town. A pond was behind our house, full of frogs, snakes, dragonflies, water skippers and even leeches. It was green with moss that felt so good between my toes when I'd wade through the mud. Bud and I built a raft out of old tree limbs. Each of us had a pole to navigate our way around the emerald-green water.

My pet duck followed me everywhere. The duck thought he was a dog and chased cars along with our neighbor's dogs. One morning, I heard a loud squawking down by the pond. A man was throwing my duck into the pond for his bird dog to retrieve! He had tied my duck's legs together. Racing down the hill, I flung myself at the man. "Stop it." I yelled. He only laughed and pushed me aside. I ran and got Dad. I'm not sure what Dad said to that horrible man but he handed over my duck and left.

Pet frogs and pollywogs filled my jars. I loved to watch the magic of the arms and legs develop on the pollywogs as their tails slowly disappeared. After they had become full-fledged frogs, I'd turn them loose. Approaching the pond one sunny day, I saw a boy with a BB gun shooting my frogs. I tore into him like a mountain lion. He knocked me into the water, and shot me in my backside with BB's before he ran off. I chased him down, tackled him and gave him a bloody nose. Dad took me to the doctor's to have the BB's extracted. I had to sit on an inner tube for a few days.

Our new house had a basement, but no laundry chute or coal furnace. Dad kept some of his law books in the basement. There were acres of hay fields behind the house and thousands of field mice in the tall hay. They were bigger than the cabin mice and had soft, brown fur and big brown, liquid eyes. They didn't run fast like the cabin mice and were easy to catch. I had a large collection of them. Having no mouse cages, I put them in the glass bookcase with Dad's law books. I couldn't wait for Dad to come home and see my mice. I had put water and cheese on each shelf. By the time he came home, the mice had nested in his books. He helped me remove them, and drove my mice and me to the country where I could release them in a place he explained would be more suitable. Dad wasn't mad. He even said I was sure a good animal trainer.

My friend saw a great horned owl on the neighbor's roof. She said owls don't see or fly well during the day, so she would help me catch it. We found a gunny-sack. Climbing up a big tree near where the owl was sitting, I slowly dropped to the roof and inched near it. She was so big and beautiful. She blinked her huge golden eyes at me as I gently placed the sack over her and tied it shut. Indians consider owls to be evil spirits. I didn't believe that. My owl was beautiful! I was told she was female because of her large size. She had a six-foot wingspan, long talons and beautiful feathers. I kept her in the garage so she could fly. I fed her hot dogs stuffed with bone meal. At first she wouldn't eat them, so I tied a string around the hot dogs and pulled them around the garage. We bonded and I considered her my lucky charm.

A biology professor at the college gave me a two-foot alligator I named Veronica. She slept with me and would not eat unless I joined her in the bath-tub to feed her chunks of raw meat. During cold winter days, she would sleep under the electric heaters in the living room. When she ventured out, she would swagger and hiss, often startling Mother's bridge club ladies. They'd take refuge by standing on the chairs. Veronica lived for six years. One summer day, as I played with her outside, a delivery truck ran over her.

Poor Mom, she should have received a reward for tolerance. I had two pet chameleons that lived on the window drapes where they ate flies. Several frogs and snakes were turned loose in the house. Often, when mom would bend over to pick up a mud clod from the carpet, it would hop away!

Wanting to earn a Girl Scout badge for a butterfly collection, but not wanting to kill them, I had a live butterfly collection in my bedroom. Many plants and a source of water were made available. The butterflies thrived and made cocoons on my walls. Watching the caterpillars emerge as beautiful butterflies was like a miracle.

Being a Girl Scout was good, but I wanted to be a Boy Scout, like Bud. Mom was his den leader so the Boy Scouts met at our house. Determined, I learned to tie all the knots, knew all the trees, hiked with them, and earned all the badges available. The Boy Scouts couldn't get rid of me. I was determined to earn enough badges to become an Eagle Scout so I could wear an Indian head-dress. When it was time to go to the National Jamboree in Valley Forge, I was eager to go. When told girls could not go, I was devastated. Bud had a wonderful time and came home with a horned lizard some Arizona scout had given him. Being a girl was not fair!

We had our annual Girl Scout Camp high in the mountains. Activities were fun and creative. Sleeping in tents, my friends and I would laugh until we were weak. Each group of scouts had a counselor. Just after taps one evening, I put a large garter snake in our counselor's sleeping bag. My friends and I had to hold our breath to keep from giggling as she climbed into her bag. She screamed as she shot out of her mummy bag! Nobody told on me but I'm sure she knew who put the snake there.

Horse standing: Cousin (left) and Dad (right).

Teaching Mike to count

2

FINALLY, I HAD MY OWN HORSE

Dad finally bought me a horse. She was perfect, a gentle bay mare named Flicka. Dad would not let me ride with a saddle, for fear I'd get hung up in the stirrup, and I was too short to jump on her, so when Flicka would lower her head to eat, I'd climb on her neck and slide down to her back. To shinny up her leg was another option. Eventually, I learned to grab her mane and swing up, Indian style. She would carry two or three of my friends behind me and we'd giggle so hard that we often fell off. We learned how to tuck and roll! Flicka would stop, being careful not to step on us. When God made an honest horse, He made Flicka!

Our family scrapbook had numerous pictures of Granddad, Dad and his sisters standing on their horses. The horses ranged from saddle horses to large, work-horses pulling wagons and thrashing machines. Dad sat a horse well and rode horseback to hunt elk or survey elk numbers for the Forest Service. One time, as he packed his saddlebags, I noticed two bottles of whiskey in one bag and poker chips and cards in the other. "What are you going to eat?" I asked. "Never mind, sister," he said. "And don't say anything to your mother."

Aunt Ruth had two gorgeous five-gaited American Saddlebred horses. She promised I could have one. The promise came true when I was eleven. Mike, a black bay gelding was mine. He was sixteen-hands tall, but by then I could mount Indian style. He was an honest horse and we soon bonded. I found some old horse-training books by Professor Berry in our basement and began teaching Mike tricks. We started with easy tricks, like shaking hands, counting and shaking his head "yes" or "no." With the help of a running W, borrowed from our milk-man Frankie, who had a team of black Percheron draft horses that pulled his milk wagon, I taught Mike how to bow, kneel, lie down and sit down. He seemed to enjoy our lessons and, when tied to the fence, he often would count or do other tricks to get my attention. After I trained Mike to lie down quietly, I'd place a large blanket over his hind-quarters. I'd lie down between his front legs and ask him to

MARINEL BOLINGER ENTERTAINS WITH TRICK HORSE — The youthful animal trainer shown with her horse, "Mike," (above) is Marinel Bolinger, who won two first places in Saturday's pet show sponsored at Bogert's grove by the Optimist Club and City Recreation Department. The horse took top honors in the "Best Trained" division, when he counted his age by pawing the ground, waved a front leg at the crowd, kneeled, played dead, and then kissed his trainer. Marinel entered four animals including "Mike;" an alligator; a "cabbit," which she said was part cat and part rabbit, and an Irish Water Spaniel, which was edged out in the homliest class by a horned toad and lizard. A daughter of Mr. and Mrs. Hal Bolinger of 1222 South Willson, Marinel appeared on the National Radio Broadcast "Welcome Traveler," in Chicago in May because of her interest in pets. She won a pet crow as a prize at that time, but the bird was killed later after being struck by a truck.

(Chronicle staff photo)

Newspaper clipping showing my Trick horse, Mike

cover us up. He'd gently reach over me, grabbing the blanket in his teeth and pulling it up to cover us both. Mike also learned to roll a barrel with his nose and dance the Schottische. My friends loved to watch Mike do his tricks. We'd have our own backyard circus and they'd bring their trick dogs. I remember when the city had an animal show for the kids. They had a pet contest. I won several ribbons that day with Mike, my alligator, and my big Irish water spaniel, Clancy.

My friends said I should join the circus but my parents thought I should be a veterinarian. By fourth-grade, I'd already decided I wanted to be a vet. I often found injured animals. Some hit by cars, some had been shot, and some I rescued from traps. I would place them in a gunny-sack and, on horseback, carry them ten miles to the veterinarian. Dad would get a monthly bill for all these little creatures, most of which I saved. I tried to get a job at the hospital to pay the bills, but they said I was too little.

Newspaper clipping of Clancy and me at the West Yellow Stone Annual Dog Derby, February, 1954

POPULARITY WENT TO CLANCY'S HEAD and the big brown Irish water spaniel ran second on the second day of the junior championship dog race at West Yellowstone as his pretty mistress, Marinel Bolinger, virtually tugged him across the finish line at Stage Coach Inn. It seems that Clancy romped home first in a field of 18 dogs Saturday and was a strong favorite Sunday. In the heat of the race, fans cheered him on, and his name was spoken over the loud speaker, which was confusing to the dog. Clancy hadn't any idea that he had acquired so many friends, but it was nice and he kept stopping along the quarter-mile runway to greet these fine people. Anyway it didn't stop Marinel from bringing home a trophy. She is the daughter of Mr. and Mrs. Hal Bolinger, of 1222 South Willson.
(Courier photo)

3

DAD BUYS A RANCH

Mom was mad, but Bud and I were thrilled when dad purchased a cattle ranch fifteen miles from town. The ranch consisted of a thousand acres of sub-irrigated grass and brush. It had an abundance of wildlife. I found many buffalo skulls. Some of the land was so swampy the horses and cattle would sink down to their backs. We didn't have to worry about irrigating, so spent our efforts building drainage ditches and burning brush. The soil consisted of peat moss and would burn in the ground for months on end. Once we had such a big fire that people could see the flames thirty miles away. I remember Granny in her cotton dress fanning out the flames with a wet gunny-sack. She must've been in her eighties by then. I loved the ranch. Helping Dad and Bud build fence was the greatest! Kitchen chores at home were dreaded. I had better things to do to help out.

Work hard and play hard, and you will live a good long life dad told us. He made sure Bud and I always worked to make our own money. After our job of selling vegetables from the garden, we collected scrap iron and hauled it across town to the Pacific Hide and Fur warehouse in our little wagon.

When I was ten, dad told Bud and me that we would be in charge of cleaning the halls of the apartment building he acquired. The apartments were on the second floor above the bakery. We also would be responsible for cleaning and repainting any vacated apartments. I left my little red wagon at the foot of the stairs. A tenant, racing down the stairs, stepped into the wagon and was propelled out into the street where he was injured. After cleaning the halls, I did not want to carry the heavy vacuum cleaner down the stairs and around to the trash, so I choose to empty it from the roof into the trash barrel. Looking down through the cloud of dirt, I saw a baker holding a huge wedding cake, now covered in the apartment hall dust I had emptied. Bud and I ran and hid in the broom closet for a long time. Not quite ready to give up on us, Dad told us to clean and repaint a vacated apartment. Having been given permission to choose the color of paint we liked, dark purple was our selection. We even painted the telephone purple. Dad would be proud of us now. Not so, we were fired and sent back to the ranch to build fence, hurrah!

Dad said not to drink water from the creek as there was a dead cow up stream. On a hot summer day my girl friend and I had run out of water while looking for the horses. A dead cow lay up stream, so we hiked to the only neighbor for a drink. I grabbed the middle wire of the neighbors' fence to crawl through. It was my most shocking experience! The barbed wire had been hooked to the main power line. I was standing in the creek and couldn't let go. I passed out! My girl friend pulled me to the bank so I wouldn't drown. I was raced to the hospital where the doctor spent several hours trying to repair my mangled hand. A legal settlement was made, as hooking the fence to the main power line was illegal. Dad said I could buy my own cows with the settlement money. I purchased thirty cows. My friend and I were to drive them fifteen miles to the ranch. Ten escaped and it took months to find them.

As my hand never healed properly, Dad made arrangements for me to go to one of the worlds top hand surgeons in Chicago. Mom and I went on the Northern Pacific Train. I loved the train. The cars were lined with Charlie Russell paintings. The seats were leather and the walls were made of hardwood. The dinning room was formal with beautiful place settings and wonderful food. Waiters and porters catered to me, as I was a kid. Mom met a friend she invited to dine with us. I had been raised to have the best of table manners, but had never seen a finger bowl. Water was served in fine china and trimmed with sliced lemon. When I picked it up and drank it, mom was so embarrassed! Her reaction left a big impression on me. I loved the sleeper compartment, the rocking motion and the train' soft whistle.

All too soon we were in Chicago at the huge hospital. The doctors and nurses were great. They spent several hours trying to save my hand by transplanting the tendons from my foot into my injured finger. I woke up with my right hand and left foot throbbing and bandaged. Given a wheel chair, I was soon driving it up and down the hall, where I met a nice man who was also in a wheel chair. He was so fun, as we had wheel chair races and became good friends. I told him all about our ranch, my animals and that I wanted to become a veterinarian. He said he had a farm in Libertyville, just outside of Chicago with many animals, and he wanted me to be his veterinarian. After a week, I was discharged from the hospital, but was told to stay near by for a month of physical therapy, as my fingers didn't bend the way they should. My friend invited me to stay at his beautiful farm until I was done with therapy. He had horses, sheep, cows and lots of dogs and cats. His house was big and wonderful. He and his help treated me like a princess. Mom had gone back home after I left the hospital. Dad, who was one of the big wigs of Montana's Republican Party, sent me a telegram that read, "Get the Hell home Sister before you get contaminated!" I did not understand it, so I showed it to Mr. Stevenson, who got a big kick out of it, saying he would like to meet my Dad. After I returned to Montana, Mr. Stevenson wrote letters to me for more than a year. Dad put Bud and me to work, tacking "I Like Ike" posters on telephone poles. Adlai Stevenson lost to Dwight D. "Ike" Eisenhower; Dad was happy.

I started seventh-grade that fall. Junior high school was not good. All the girls talked about were clothes and boys. The boys were growing faster than me, so I stopped fighting with them. For the first time, I didn't like school. I had to walk five miles, even in the freezing cold. Taking home-making class, I made an ugly purple skirt. In cooking class, I spilled boiling candy on my injured hand resulting in huge, painful blisters. I tried to play the clarinet

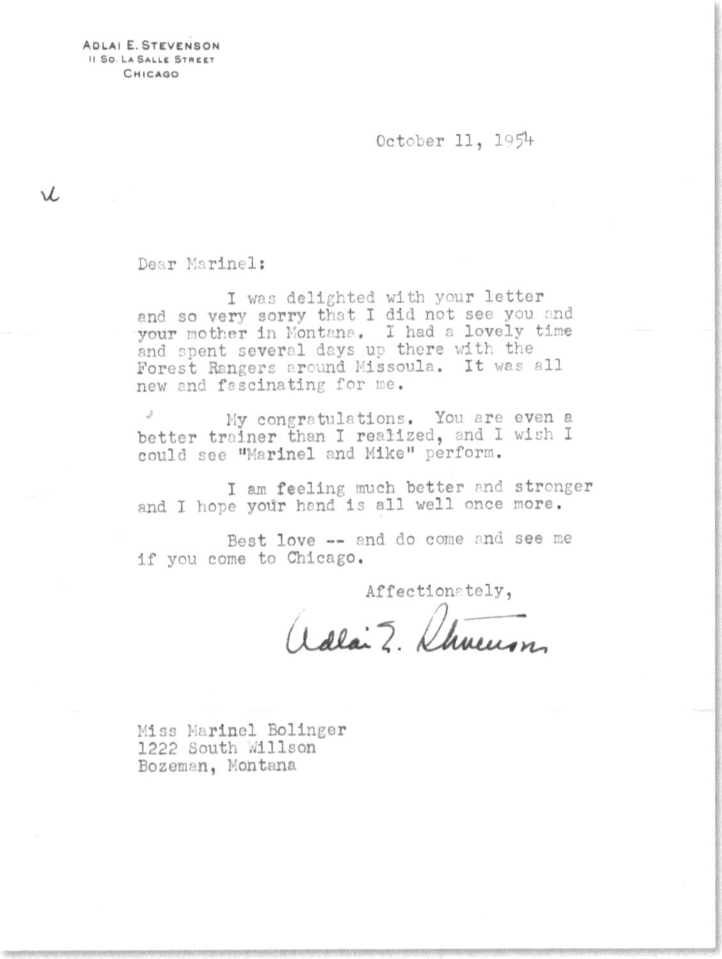

ADLAI E. STEVENSON
11 So. LA SALLE STREET
CHICAGO

October 11, 1954

Dear Marinel:

I was delighted with your letter
and so very sorry that I did not see you and
your mother in Montana. I had a lovely time
and spent several days up there with the
Forest Rangers around Missoula. It was all
new and fascinating for me.

My congratulations. You are even a
better trainer than I realized, and I wish I
could see "Marinel and Mike" perform.

I am feeling much better and stronger
and I hope your hand is all well once more.

Best love -- and do come and see me
if you come to Chicago.

Affectionately,

Adlai E. Stevenson

Miss Marinel Bolinger
1222 South Willson
Bozeman, Montana

Letter from Adlai Stevenson, October, 1954

in band. My teacher said I sounded like a sick chicken, so I quit. My good
grades dropped lower and lower. Some girls thought they were movie stars;
they called me Bud's little brother. I showed them. I beat them up on their
way home from school. Dad got a call from a parent who said I'd just beat up
his daughter and four other girls. His reply: "Too bad my daughter weighs
half as much as yours." I think he was proud of me.

We took dance lessons for P.E. All the boys would line up on one side of
the gym and the girls on the other. The principal would blow her whistle and

the boys would have to ask us to dance. I had a lot more boys for friends than girls, but I really didn't want to dance with them.

Summers in Montana are special. Because the state is far to the north, the evenings are long. We played baseball or went swimming in the river for several hours after dinner. Sometimes, we saw the Northern Lights. Kids from my junior high class would come by to visit. Some of them said they were going steady. The first time a boy tried to hold my hand, I told him to let go of my "toe fingers." He didn't understand, but let go. Little did he know my toe tendons had been transplanted into my fingers. This was a great excuse for not having to hold a boy's hand and I used it for a long time.

I was not one to hang out and talk about boys, trash other girls with catty remarks or worry about the latest fashions. One of the worst days of my life was when my mother came home with twin dresses. One for me, one for her! She insisted we wear them downtown. I was forced to hold her hand as she paraded us down one side of Main Street and up the other. Several girls from the junior high school saw us and started jeering. I wanted to crawl down a sewer drain! Shortly after that humiliating episode, the science teacher asked me to bring my alligator to science class. One of those girls asked if she could pet it and I said "of course." Veronica had never bitten anyone before but, that day, justice was served. She nailed her hand and wouldn't let go! I finally freed the screaming girl. "Now you know what it feels like to be hurt," I said.

My animals, especially my horse, were my sanctuary. Dad gave Flicka to a little girl for her first horse and her parents asked me to teach her how to ride. I was proud to be a riding instructor. Flicka had a good, new home and was again a babysitter horse. Since I was older, Dad said I needed a bigger, faster horse and keeping Mike was just right. He could stay in the back yard in town as long as he had feed. When fall came, Dad said Mike would have to winter at the ranch. Mike liked corn stalks. The neighbors let me take theirs. Collecting bundles from friends' gardens, I carried them home on Mike. If I could collect enough, maybe Dad would let me keep Mike in town all winter. One evening, my friends and I found a haystack a few blocks from home. We spent the evening sliding down it. As we left, I picked up an armful of hay and carried it home to Mike. Late that night, there was a knock on the door. It was our friend, Sheriff Don. He asked what I'd been feeding Mike. I was afraid he thought Mike wasn't getting enough food so I told him about all the corn stalks and the arm full of hay. Dad asked what Don wanted. "The neighbor behind you called and said his hay stack was ruined and someone had stolen some hay. He asked me to investigate," Don said. "I followed a hay trail to your house." I was so scared. Maybe I'd have to go to jail. "I know that man," Dad said. "He's a bad neighbor and he almost killed her pet duck." Sheriff Don gave Dad a wink and told me he wouldn't arrest me this time, but be careful to never steal again. The corncobs ran out and Mike had to go to the ranch to winter. Dad said he could come back when the first dandelions bloomed.

Winters come early in Montana. We often had our first snow on Labor Day. In October, Montana dresses in bright shades of red and gold. Indian summer prevails. In November, she embraces the heavy snows and cold. I loved all the seasons.

I was becoming a good skier and welcomed the snows. The ski hills would open by Thanksgiving Day. The snow lay soft and deep in the forest and even in town. Before we had a ski hill near Bozeman, I'd go to the town

of West Yellowstone to ski. The temperature was often thirty degrees below zero or colder. The ride up the chair tow was cold. One time, the chair tow stopped half way up the mountain. After a freezing hour in the chair, we were told we'd have to jump out. It was a long jump down, but the deep snow cushioned the fall. I'd thrown my skis down before jumping. After digging my way out and finding my skis, I went to the Stage Coach Inn for hot chocolate by the big fireplace, tired and happy.

There were several ponds at the ranch. Dad built a duck blind in one. When Clancy heard the word "ducks", he'd race to the closet where Dad and Bud kept their guns and lick the gun-stocks. We'd load up the decoys, guns, some food and head for the duck blind. I pretended to like duck hunting, so I wouldn't have to stay home, but it wasn't my favorite activity. It was so cold, having to sit absolutely still in the blind, waiting for the ducks to fly in. Dad and Bud would open fire. Clancy would plunge into the freezing water and carry the poor mallards back to the blind, where their necks were rung as Clancy would shake freezing water over my already half-frozen body.

I'd trained Clancy to pull my toboggan around town. He was good until he got into a fight with another dog. I'd fly out of the sled as we both became tangled in the harness. Nearly everyone in town knew Clancy. Some neighbors didn't like him, as he'd carry milk cartons off their porch to our house. One Thanksgiving he carried home a large stuffed turkey.

We heard there were to be a sled dog races in West Yellowstone that winter, with a special race for kids. Several teams of dogs were coming from Alaska and Canada for the race. They were parachuted in just south of West Yellowstone. People arrived from all over. There was a huge gathering of dogs, kids and spectators. To see the dogs, their drivers and sleds being parachuted to the snow below was amazing. I entered Clancy in the kids' race. It was to be down the main snow-packed road to town. The others, all boys, were racing their lead husky dogs. Only one other racer had a hunting dog. I had the most unusual one. Clancy, my Irish Water Spaniel was very big, liver brown, with curly coat and a rat tail. About 15 of us lined up at the starting line. When the starters' gun went off, I yelled "Ducks, Clancy!" Away we flew. The huskies had their noses to the ground, digging into the snow for traction. Clancy held his head high, looking for ducks. We passed all the huskies. Clancy had a big fan club. "Go Clancy!" they yelled. This distracted him and he made three detours to greet his fans. If he'd not been distracted, we would've won by a large margin. We still finished second and fans and reporters gathered around. The next day, Clancy and I made front-page headlines in several newspapers.

Spring was soon to come. A Chinook blew in the lovely smell of melting snow and fragrant pines. Icicles began to drip. A few daffodils reared their yellow heads through the melting snow. Montana skies are seldom gray. They're "do or don't skies." Mostly they were a beautiful blue, with puffy, white clouds. When they were not full of sunshine, they were filled with soft, dancing snowflakes in the winter or raindrops in the summer. It was an all-or-nothing sky that embraced a million stars. Summer thunderstorms were intense with wild lightning, bouncing off the mountainsides. Then the storms would be over. There were no depressing tunnels of gray. Whatever the sky decided to do, it did it with conviction and then turned to a new page and to another new sky. Thus, Montana became known as Big Sky Country. From this big sky, I learned a valuable life lesson: Don't get trapped in a gray tunnel. Get out, shut the door and move forward to something new and positive. It laid the groundwork for my resilience that became my key to survival.

As the snow was melting, I looked forward to summertime riding. During the winter, I'd practically memorized the Horsemen's Encyclopedia. I knew the breed characteristics of every horse, including all the draft horses. I learned that all horses, except some draft horses, traced their origins back two thousand years to the Arabian horse. To my knowledge, there was only one Arabian horse in Montana and that was a remount stallion whose sire, Witez 11 had been imported to the United States during World War II by General George Patton. The government had used Arabian stallions to breed with other breeds of horses, especially the thoroughbred, according to the thoroughbred stud-books. These government-owned stallions were called remount stallions. The one I knew was a big, black bay stallion, athletic and gentle. He was nearly thirty years old and died that spring.

I asked my parents if I could use the money I'd made to buy an Arabian stallion. Mom said stallions were too dangerous, but Dad thought it was a good idea. He had several mares at the ranch and wanted to raise some foals. We found an Arabian horse breeder in Wyoming who had several two-year-old colts. A big grey caught our attention: He was fifteen hands or taller with big, strong bones. Seldom handled, he appeared to have an honest attitude. Dad and I loaded him into our little homemade horse trailer and hauled him home. We unloaded him at the railroad shipping corrals that evening. Excited and happy, I could hardly sleep. The next morning I ran two miles to the shipping corrals. He walked quietly up to me. I slipped my lead rope onto his halter and slowly led him around the corral. I rubbed his long arched neck and his short strong back. He let me rub his beautiful head and small tipped ears. When I took the lead rope off, he followed me. I sat on the corral fence, letting him sniff me, as he rubbed his head on my leg. He seemed relaxed and curious. "I know I can ride him," I thought. "Won't Dad be surprised?" I snapped the lead rope on his halter again, rubbed his head and gently blew into his nostrils. He was tall, so mounting him would be by means of the corral fence. I gently slid onto his back. He turned his head to nuzzle my foot. I put no pressure on him, but let him walk around the corral. I couldn't believe how gentle he was. This was the first horse I'd ever trained by myself! Now all I needed was quiet time. The next day I rubbed my stallion's legs and picked up his front hoofs. As I curried him all over, he seemed to like the attention. I slid on his back again. Once more, he turned and sniffed my foot. I put light pressure on his sides and clucked for him to move forward. He responded and soon we were trotting around the corral. When I gently pulled back on the halter lead line, he stopped. I invited Mom and Dad to the corral at noon, for a surprise. When I slid on his back and trotted him around, they were surprised indeed. "We thought it'd take several weeks for you to break him," Dad said. To that, I replied, "I'm not breaking him, we're learning together and we both like it."

When I bought this wonderful horse, I was told his registered name was Hut Hitan, which translates to "whale" in Arabic. He got the name because of his size. Dad still would not let me ride with a saddle, which was fine. I loved riding bareback and was soon swinging onto his back from his mane. I rode him nearly every day. My girlfriends and I all rode together and formed the Alley Brigade. Racing up and down the alleys, we'd pick apples from the overhanging branches. I rode Hitan to the cemetery where I jumped back and forth over Granddad's grave. I knew Granddad would be proud, as he had been an avid horseman. My gelding, Mike, became my ranch horse that summer and I rode him when I helped Dad build fence. Hitan stayed behind our house in town all summer and winter.

Hitan was fast and had a lot of endurance. I raced my friends on their horses and always won. Endurance racing had not yet become a sport. If it had, I'm sure my horse would've been a champion. One day, I found a lovely green meadow with a sparkling creek running through it. Shaded by pine trees, I stretched out on the grass and watched the big puffy clouds roll through the sky. Hitan would graze nearby, nuzzling me with his soft muzzle. I dreamed we were riding through the blue heavens. I was lucky to have this great horse and wrote a poem about him:

> "I love the wonderful horse, with beauty splendid and rare.
> It may be a stallion or gelding, it may be a filly or mare.
> I love to feel the hardened muscles, beneath me as I ride.
> Strong and swift and graceful, are his even stride.
> I do not mind the flowing mane that lashes at my face.
> I love his long and flowing tail, arched proudly as we race.
> Yes, the wonderful horse, with beauty, endurance and speed.
> It makes me feel like I own the world, to ride this beautiful steed."

Mom and Dad seemed to fight more and more. My bedroom was just down the hall and we shared a common bathroom. I could hear them yelling. Mom did not want any part of the ranch and was mad at Dad for buying it. Dad also had gold mines in Montana and Colorado. She was mad because he didn't strike it rich. One summer, Bud and his friend went to Colorado to work the gold mine. They had a great adventure, but never struck it rich. Dad had someone make a gold nugget out of brass. He gave it to Mom to keep her from being upset about the mines. She proudly showed it to all her friends. When she found out it wasn't real, she got even madder. Dad brought mercury home from his mines, and Bud and I would play with it for hours. He also retrieved a nickel slot machine from the Elks Club when Montana outlawed gambling. We let our friends play it and made some spending money.

Some nights I couldn't stand hearing my parents fight. I would grab my mummy-bag, crawl out of my window and run away on Hitan. I wasn't afraid of the fields or woods at night as long as Hitan was near. I'd return by early morning and crawl back through the window. My parents never knew I'd been gone.

Grandmother Nell, Mom's domineering mother, would make Bud and I read Dante's Inferno with her. We hated that book. It had horrible pictures of naked men burning in hell in it. She said we'd go to hell if we weren't good. My other grandmother was gentle and patient. She'd take us to Sunday school. She loved ranching, and lived into her nineties.

When winter came, Dad gave me his Navy waterproof parka with wolf fur lining. If fit me like a tent. I always rode bareback so the body heat of my horse filled the parka and kept me warm. We loved to run through the deep snow. Hitan would play with me in the snow when he was turned loose in the pasture. We'd chase each other through the snow-drifts. He would rear up when I rolled in the snow, and lightly dance around me. Dad was shocked when he saw us playing like that. He couldn't believe it. I told him we often enjoyed horse-play!

Mom was worried. I think she feared I'd turn into a horse or maybe a frog. She decided to intervene. She signed Bud and me up for piano lessons with the Catholic nuns. For five long years, we took piano lessons. The only songs I liked, and can still remember, were Stephen Foster's songs. We were forced to play in recitals, on stage, by ourselves, with lots of people watching. It was terrifying. I had to wear a long gown and curtsy to the audience when I finished playing. Bud had to wear a suit and tie and bow to the audience.

Mom made me walk around the house with a book on my head. I learned to iron Dad's shirts, set the perfect formal dinner table, serve her bridge parties and take dancing lessons. Actually, I liked the tap dancing. I didn't want to take ballet because it seemed so prissy. Recitals were the worst part of dancing lessons, especially when I had to wear a tutu onstage.

Bud roared when he saw me. He showed no mercy. I wanted to leap off the stage and punch him in the nose!

What Bud and I really liked, when we weren't outside, was listening to our parents' records. Nobody had TVs then. We liked the Western classics like "Old Shep," "The Strawberry Roan," "Sam Bass," "Behind These Old Prison Walls," "Old Dan Tucker," "My Home's in Montana," and "Cattle Call." I even liked Broadway musicals and knew nearly every word of all these songs. Bud and I sang the wonderful old Western songs together until the year he died.

When I was in seventh grade, Bud was a freshman in high school. His friends often came to our house since they could play poker in his basement bedroom. I was not allowed to join them. "No skirts allowed," Bud would yell. They were chewing tobacco and spitting it on his wall. I was glad I had my horse to run to.

Bud was learning to drive. Mom and Dad had two couples over for dinner and I had set the table. Bud sat next to me and had his elbow on the table. "Boy, is he going to get in trouble for those bad manners," I thought. Suddenly, A large pool of blood began to seep onto the white, lace tablecloth. I was afraid to say anything. When Dad saw it, he yelled, "What the hell?" Bud said nothing, but his face was turning white. Dad jumped up and grabbed him out of his chair. "What happened?" he demanded. Bud replied, "I had my elbow out the window when I was driving and a car hit it." We took his shirt off. Blood spurted everywhere. Mom and another lady nearly fainted. The end of Bud's elbow was nearly gone! Dad had always said," If you stick your elbow out too far, it'll go home in another man's car."

Marinel (left) and Jackie (right)

4

HIGH SCHOOL

Eighth grade was somewhat like seventh grade. I was anxious to go to high school. While taking piano lessons from the nuns, I met a nice Irish girl named Jackie. She had long, raven-black hair and bright blue eyes. She was not only beautiful, but she was nice too! We became best friends and still are today. The Catholic school had classes only through eighth grade, so Jackie started high school with me as a freshman. Bud was now a senior. I felt important because I knew most of the upper classmen. They still couldn't get rid of me!

High school classes were more interesting than junior high and the extracurricular activities were fun. I joined art club, ski club, rifle club and concert choir, and earned a place on the girls ski team. The Bridger Bowl ski hill opened sixteen miles from town. The school and town enthusiastically supported our ski team. During ski season, team members were let out of class early and bused to the mountain. There were four girls and seven boys on the team. We competed in downhill, slalom and giant slalom racing. We raced down different mountains around Montana and at Jackson Hole,

Wyoming. Our skis were long, as high as we could reach. Safety bindings had not been invented; our "long thong bindings" were long leather straps wrapped around our ankles several times. We waxed our skis and sharpened their edges before each competition. Downhill racing was a thrill and my favorite event. It meant going nearly straight down the mountain as fast as possible. The speed was sixty to seventy miles per hour over bumps or "moguls" that often propelled us high in the air. Even with goggles, the wind would tear up my eyes. When the snow was soft, we'd fight the ruts left by previous racers. When the hill was icy, we went all that much faster. If we fell, we'd fall a long ways. The steeper the hill, the less impact the fall and, though the distance was long, the finish line seemed to come fast. After the race, I'd think of all the places I could've made better time and wish I could immediately rerun the race. Later, I'd think of the dangers I'd passed and wonder if I were crazy to love this sport!

There was one older girl from another town who loved to scare us at the starting gate. She'd sing this song as we waited for our turn:

> *"There was blood on her bindings.*
> *There was blood on her skis.*
> *Her intestinal fortitude*
> *Was scattered through the trees.*
> *We picked her up*
> *And laid her down*
> *And poured her out of her boots*
> *And she ain't going to ski no more!"*

While racing downhill, on an icy course in Helena, I fell hard. The fall knocked the wind out of my sails and the ski patrol toboggan took me down the rest of the mountain. The hundred-mile car ride home was painful. X-rays showed I had a compression fracture of the thoracic vertebrae. One of our boys suffered a broken leg. I healed without surgery. That same year an Idaho high school racer broke her back and became a paraplegic. They made a movie about her and when people would tell me the sport was too dangerous, I'd say, "You could get run over by a bus!"

We had a great high school principal. He'd come to my class and had me excused to go skiing with him. Each summer, he'd take five girls on a two-week pack trip through one of Montana's great wilderness areas. I was always included. These trips were spectacular. I'd always ride Mike. He loved to swim and could cross those high mountain lakes like a moose. I'd either stay astride or slip off into the water and hang on to his tail. All the girls were in the rifle club; one was a national rifle champion. We always saw lots of bears, especially grizzlies. On one trip, in the Bob Marshall Wilderness near Glacier Park, we made camp near the famous Chinese Wall. We were near a glacier and saw numerous large bear tracks. It was too late to ride farther and we were apprehensive about the fresh bear tracks. Building an extra-large fire we kept it burning all night. Tying our ropes together we formed a circle around us and around our horses. We hung cans and anything else that would rattle on the rope. Staying up all night, we listened to the bears circling our camp. The horses were nervous, stomping the ground, while tied to their picket line. Finally, daylight came. We thought it unwise to cook breakfast, so broke camp early and saddled up. The bears had left many new tracks. Still nervous, the horses were anxious to hit the trail. The next day, we saw a forest ranger. He said two men had camped where we had camped the night before. The grizzle bears had killed both men.

Having spent a lot of time in Montana's wilderness areas, I have seen dozens of grizzlies. We were taught to stay calm and to talk or sing. Bears are short sighted, but have a great sense of smell and hearing. While riding behind a string of pack mules, I saw a large grizzly on a hill above us. It came roaring down the mountain and, with one swipe of its huge claws it ripped open a pack mule's abdomen, then charged on down the slope. The mule died of shock within a few minutes. My closest encounter with a grizzly was near Yellowstone Park. For two summers, I was the pack trip cook for a guest ranch. One trip was for a man and his son who wanted to photograph grizzlies for two weeks. We had seen many bears the first week. Upon topping a ridge, we were met by a large scar-faced grizzly sow with three cubs. She reared up on her hind legs and swayed back and forth with a furious growl as her grizzled, silver fur flowed down off her massive shoulders. There were five of us. I wondered which one of us she would charge first. She was not more than twenty feet away. To our relief, she dropped down on all fours and ambled into the forest with her three cubs.

In 1958, Montana had a severe earthquake near the town of West Yellowstone. Many people were buried alive the day the mountain fell on their campsite near what is now called Quake Lake. A friend of mine was fishing nearby. That night he was sleeping in his overhead camper. Suddenly, the camper began to sway and shake. Certain a grizzly had scaled his camper, he climbed through the trucks back window into the driver's seat and drove forward and backward, slamming his brakes on and off, trying to dislodge the bear. The camper stopped jerking and Ed went back to sleep. The next morning he discovered he was teetering on a fault line, being one of the lucky ones who had survived the quake.

High school years were some of the best years of my life. Summers were never boring. We kept busy with outdoor theaters, timber parties, slumber parties, floating the rivers, fishing, horseback riding, camping, cruising the drag, dances, baseball, cabin parties and, best of all, the dump outside of town of West Yellowstone. Yes, the dump. We'd drive up the canyon to the dump to see the bears. Six to eight of us would cram into an old car and drive to the dump before it got dark. We'd roll down the window and, if a bear stuck its head through the window, we'd punch it in the nose then roll up the window as fast as possible. The person who actually touched the bear would get ten points and a beer. First came the black bears, then finally the grizzlies would arrive, scattering all the other bears. The grizzlies would fight over the garbage and when they approached the car, some would crawl on the hood or even the top. We'd scream and laugh as the car rolled back and forth. The dump closed my senior year and our close encounters were curtailed.

During my high school years, we drank a little beer and played a few pranks, but drugs were not even considered. We had "Queer's Day" every Thursday, which meant we wore green to school. No one had any idea why, or what a queer was. It was just a tradition. There were 180 in my graduating class and most of them were nice. I don't remember any bullying since eighth-grade. Jackie and I made a point of spending time with our classmates who were shy or a little different.

Cruising the drag was a must, as was drag racing. We'd cruise from one end of Main Street to the other. The drive-in at the south end of Main Street made a great turn-around place for our next lap. Honking and waving to the passengers in the next car jump-started our social skills. Gas was twenty-five cents a gallon.

Pranks were common, but usually harmless. Most occurred in the evenings, especially during slumber parties. Collecting beer cans and dumping them on the mayor's lawn, moving the picnic tables from the park into the street, letting air out of a friend's tires or ringing doorbells, then hiding were favorites. I frequently rang the doorbell of a girlfriend's house. Her dad was big and mean. He'd kicked my dog, so I loved to torment him. As I ran to hide, he jumped out of the bushes and grabbed me. His wife called the sheriff. I was so scared when they placed me in the patrol car's back seat that I wet my pants. The sheriff drove me home. Dad and the sheriff looked at each other and shook their heads.

At the summer rodeos in small nearby towns we provided cheering for our local cowboys as they rode for glory. Jackie and I enjoyed dancing in the old western bars and visiting with the old sheepherders and old cowboys. I had taught her the words to every western song Bud and I had learned, just as she had taught me the words to many Irish songs. Much to the delight of these old sheepherders, cowboys, loggers and miners, we entertained them with our great songs. Most of the sheepherders were of Irish decent and joined in the song-fest.

Many of my classmates and I drank beer. Most of our parents were drinkers, maybe because they'd all gone through prohibition. While in high school, Dad and his friend had made moonshine whiskey on an island in the Gallatin River and sold it to hotel guests on their way to West Yellowstone. Dad's

LEANING AROUND THE BARREL — Miss Marinel Bolinger, 17, daughter of Mr. and Mrs. Hal Bolinger, takes her Arabian stallion, "Hut Hitan," around one of the barrels in the girls' barrel race at the JayCee Rodeo in the Montana State College fieldhouse. She graduated from Bozeman high school in June and plans to enter Colorado State at Denver this fall.
Chronicle photo

Barrel racing with Hut Hitan

father, the judge, found out. The story goes that Granddad wasn't upset his son was selling moonshine, although he was a non-drinker, he also was against prohibition. He was upset that the whiskey had been watered down. Granddad viewed the dishonesty of diluting the whiskey as pure fraud. He punished Dad by taking him out of high school his senior year, and sending him to run the sheep ranch for a year before he could graduate.

There was, and still is, an old brick bar called Stacy's. It is ten miles from town, near Dad's old moonshine still. It was the favorite hangout for my parents, my friends and me. It's a true western bar, owned by good western folks. The horseshoe-shaped bar is ideal for conversations. The hardwood floor is nearly worn out from the hundreds of western dances. The walls are covered with authentic local photos of the wildest of the wild west, like the one of a buffalo plunging off a diving board into a pool of water. A photo of an elk trained to pack deer and bear out of the wilderness always intrigued me and we all took pride in the photos of Montana's World Champion All-Around Cowboys. Some say Montana is the last best place—home to hard-working and hard-playing folks. I agree. Bar room brawls seem to be the state's most popular sport. It would be a rare night if there weren't several fights. After the fights end, the two men usually shake hands and buy a round of drinks. Everyone looks forward to Saturday night dances at the bar. Six days of hard ranch work make it a popular place. Since it is not located within the town limits, the police are not involved. The local sheriff seldom shows. His main concern is that everyone gets home safely, either by horseback, truck or tractor. I have never missed a high school class reunion, which usually ends up at this bar where we reminisce about the good old days, and the dancing we have done to help wear out the old hardwood floor.

Timber and river parties were weekend high school retreats. The guys would bring a keg or two and we'd build a bonfire, cook our food and drink beer. If the sheriff arrived, we'd scatter like quail. To my knowledge, nobody was ever caught and nobody was ever involved in an accident more serious than barbwire cuts and torn clothes after running from the sheriff.

Periodically, a group of girls who called themselves the Zombies' would travel a hundred miles to our town for a rumble. We were told to meet them at Beer Bottle Bend. I'd stopped fighting in sixth grade and there were no gangs in our school. Each Zombie wore a beer can opener around her neck as proof of gang membership. These girls from Butte were big and mean and they'd cut us with those can openers. I was glad I was a fast runner and a good tree climber. I had better things to do than rumble.

I'd been elected one of two cheerleaders from the sophomore class and looked forward to joining the squad that next fall. On Labor Day weekend, I rode Mike to the cabin and tied him to a tree for the night. For three years, I'd been mounting him by running up behind him, placing my hands on his rump and vaulting onto his back, like Roy Rogers. That morning, I rushed down the hill, intending to do my vault. Mike must've been sleeping. I startled him and he kicked me in the face. I woke up in the hospital with multiple fractures of the jaw and four front teeth missing! The doctor couldn't wire my jaw, so my head was placed in a plaster cast. Only my eyes, nose and mouth were visible. I was hospitalized for several days. My high school principal brought my old brown pack-trip hat adorned with flowers, just like I always did with wildflowers when we went on pack trips. What a sight I must've been on the football field sidelines! I couldn't open my mouth for eight weeks and, to top it all off, I got the mumps! The swelling had nowhere to go but into my face. I recovered after two months and I finally

got to enjoy being a cheerleader. My pet hawk was the team mascot. During one football game, he left his perch and headed for the middle of the field. I ran after him, through the players, as did the referees. The radio announcer delighted in his play-by-play call: "There's a fowl on the ten yard line, now it's on the forty yard line . . ."

Boys were looking more interesting to me now. The host school would have dances after our out-of-town football and basketball games. A couple of good-looking Butte boys asked Jackie and me to dance. They combed their hair back into duck-tails and had cigarette packs rolled up the sleeves of their T-shirts. They were great dancers. The one I liked called himself Evil Knievel. Jackie liked his pal, Awful Knofel. The Butte girls were not happy to see them dancing with us. Evil and Awful came to Bozeman to see us, pulling up in front of my house on two huge, noisy motorcycles. Evil asked if I'd like to go for a spin around the block with him. I didn't like motorcycles, but agreed to go if he went slow and just around the block. Still a little shy around boys, I didn't want to snuggle up too close to him, so I sat on the back fender instead of the seat. Evil took off fast and headed for the highway. He drove 20 miles at full speed. The fender was so hot. I felt I was on fire! I screamed. Evil thought I was laughing and didn't stop. When we reached my house, I was in tears and he couldn't believe I'd been on the fender, not the seat. Treated for third-degree burns at the hospital, I had to sit on an inner tube for two weeks.

Our school had dances after home games too. I still had a crush on my fourth grade boyfriend, Howie. He was the football quarterback and a star basketball player. It was easy to cheer for him. We had fun fishing, rafting and hunting and he gave me his letter sweater, senior ring, and later an engagement ring. He had the hottest car on the drag—the movie "Grease" had nothing over us! So this was why girls liked boys, I thought. I was a late bloomer but not too late. We would double date. Blueberry Hill was our secret spot. Necking was okay, anything below the neck was not. Boy, could we steam up the car windows and even melt the ice off the mirrors!

I liked art and decorating and often was chosen to pick the theme and decorations for our dances. I went all out for the senior prom: a romantic full moon hung above a garden wall. There were stars shining on the palm trees and a waterfall made of blue crepe paper. I wore my blue, strapless formal. Howie wore his white sports coat, a pink carnation and black-and-white saddle shoes. He was so handsome. We all danced with our special guys. It was heavenly. The principal had told us we couldn't turn the lights down low and I got confused when I felt something hard in Howie's front pants pocket. "Why'd you bring your flashlight to the dance?" I asked. He didn't respond but, as I learned five years later at a class reunion, every guy in school had heard about my comment!

My parents knew we had beer parties. Dad said if we were going to party, he preferred we party at our house or cabin. Driving and drinking was not allowed. Our cabin was everyone's favorite. One winter we decided to have a party there. The snow was three-feet deep. We had to walk two miles to get the keg to the cabin and the toboggan was nowhere in sight. So we wrapped the keg in Dad's new Pendleton bathroom and pulled it up the steep, snowy hill. Upon reaching the cabin, the guys hoisted the keg into the kitchen sink. The sink broke and the beer keg and dads' new robe fell through. Bud and his friends had come to the cabin for their own party. Again Bud and I shared memories.

I invited my friends to a party at our house in town. We'd never had hard liquor before. Mom and Dad were gone to their own party. Some one brought bottles of sloe gin. The girls liked it because it was sweet and a pretty pink color. The guys liked it because it was something new. We liked it a lot, but it didn't like us. The front yard was covered in a fresh blanket of snow. By morning, the snow was mostly pink. Dry heaves were the worst! What looked and tasted so good became nightmare. High school kids were passed out throughout the house. Mom and Dad came home and went to bed without seeing the pink snow or the passed-out teenagers. One girl crawled into Mom and Dad's bed and snuggled up between them. A boy crawled into the back seat of my Dad's car and passed out. As Dad drove to work the next morning, Doug rose up and yelled, "This isn't the cabin." Dad nearly drove into a light pole and came close to a heart attack.

Dad still insisted Bud and I work. He informed us that he was building a Frost Top root beer and hamburger establishment across from the high school in order to establish a new zoning law for a client. Bud and I were to run it for two years. Bud was in college, but I still had my junior and senior years of high school ahead of me. Leslie, my special ski friend from Helena said she would help. We hired high schools best looking girls and dressed them in "skorts" a combination of very short skirts and shorts. We put together a loud stereo system for our favorite music and flooded the town with free root beer coupons. We were ready to open, though neither Bud nor I, nor any of our help had ever experienced working in a drive-in hamburger stand. Opening night, hundreds of cars filled the parking lot. The root beer, unknown to Bud and I should have been diluted fifty times. We served the straight syrup. In the excitement and haste of the "grand opening" many hamburgers were served with out the meat. A screw fell into a hamburger bun, and broke a customers tooth. The car-hops were overwhelmed. Family friends walked to the window to return money the car-hops had dropped. The popcorn machine caught on fire creating such a thick cloud of smoke, that the help inside could barely see. Customers were yelling and blowing their horns. By midnight the crowd dispersed and we collapsed into a fit of laughter. "Why did dad want us to do this? He would not allow us to end in failure, so insisted we continue for one more year.

The high school fired our principal because he was too nice to us and hired a stern, mean principal. He in turn hired a truant officer to keep order over his young subjects. We named the truant officer "Freddy the Field Mouse." For the slightest infarction of the new strict rules, the truant officer would notify the parents of the offender, insisting they be grounded and at home by eight o'clock each night. Only if they had a night job, could they remain out past their curfew time. Every offender applied to work for Bud and me until their probation time had been served. By the end of the first summer we turned two hundred W-2 forms into my dads' office for tax accounting. Freddy sat outside our establishment every night to check on his inmates. We all started to enjoy this game of cat and mouse. The high school students rebelled against the strict new rules. We dressed in black and white prison striped clothing and some students handcuffed themselves to their lockers, insisting on the reinstatement of our former and nice principal, the one who took us skiing and on pack trips. We never won the stand off, but at least our old principal knew how much we cared for him and the new one knew how much he was disliked. The next school year was the same. We were the towns' most popular employers. Unknown to me, a Saturday night employee emptied two bottles of vodka into the orange juice dispenser. Church-goers stopping by for a Sunday treat got more than they bargained for.

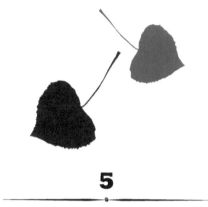

5

THE SCATTERING OF LOVED ONES

Shortly after high school graduation, our parents told Bud and me they were getting a divorce. None of my friends' parents were divorced. In fact, divorce was seldom heard of in our circles. They'd waited for both Bud and me to finish high school, probably thinking it would be easier for us, but it wasn't. Everyone in town was talking about it. Friends of the family were choosing sides. Dad paid my mother to move out of the state. She was lost for a long time and never recovered her self-esteem. She was always too nice; she had been a "door mat" as people took advantage of her. Perhaps her overbearing mother had made her that way. We were sad and confused. Bud looked at me with sad, honest blue eyes and said, "Sister, when the going gets tough the tough get going."

Dad was nice, but was a strong individual and highly respected. When he said jump, Bud and I would ask how high. As an attorney, he was popular with the ranchers and farmers. He was versatile and resilient, but the trait I admired most was his respect and kindness to the common people. After work he would often go to the old town bars where he had hundreds of friends, many were quite poor. He did a lot of pro-bono work. He didn't like to mix with the country club set; social status was not of concern to him. This is a trait I definitely inherited from him.

I wanted to go to college in Montana but was sent to Colorado for pre-vet studies. I'm sure this move was to keep me out of the middle of the divorce. I didn't like college in Colorado. Mom wanted me to join a sorority, so reluctantly I went through rush and pledged Pi Beta Phi. My roommate wanted to join a sorority, but none would take her. She was crushed. I realized the cruelty of this fraternal system and didn't like people being excluded because of their looks, personality or any personal characteristic unless it was dishonesty. Being in a sorority was not for me.

The best part of college in Colorado was that I got to bring my Arabian stallion Hitan with me. I rode with the rodeo team and the horse quadrille. I also was on the ski team. I studied hard, determined to get good grades that would help me get into veterinary school. The other plus side of Colorado was that my best friend Jackie was going to Colorado Women's College in Denver.

Jackie and I would make the trip from Montana to Colorado together. We were told not to pick up strangers. We had a friend from West Yellowstone who asked if she could ride with us. She had a pistol with her. I'd fallen asleep in the back seat when the car suddenly stopped. Several bikers who were Hell's Angels had stopped us and were looking in the windows. We'd heard of Hell's Angels out of California and locked the doors. They persisted in talking to us, something about a car going over the bank. They said a man in the car was hurt and asked if we'd take him to the nearest hospital, in Cheyenne, as we were going south and they were headed north. We were unsure of the situation until the bikers hauled the disoriented man up the bank. We agreed to take him to Cheyenne. He smelled of whiskey and appeared extremely intoxicated. Not knowing if he was safe or if he might turn on us, we blindfolded him, put him in the front seat and held the loaded pistol to his head. For two hours, Jackie drove, he swayed back and forth, and Sara and I took turns holding the gun on him! We got to the hospital, opened the passenger door and he fell out against the curb. I yelled at a nurse to get a doctor and we drove off.

Jackie and I decided to go home for Christmas. The radio said a severe winter storm was closing in. We scoffed. We were from Montana. A little snow never bothered us. Somewhere south of Casper, Wyoming, the winds began howling and a blinding blizzard raged. It was a white out. We couldn't see the road. It was twenty-five degrees below zero. We had to keep moving or we would freeze to death. This stretch of highway was closed; our gas gauge registered low. Our only chance was for one of us to drive and the other to walk ahead of the car to find the highway. If we survived, it would be a miracle. After taking turns walking and driving, I thought I saw a light in the distance. It was an old gas station and it was closed. We plowed through the deep snow and knocked on the door. After several minutes we were greeted by a 12-gauge shotgun, held by a grizzled old man! He finally let us in and built a fire in his pot-belly stove. Jackie's brand-new coat burst into flames. I put it out. We were so cold and hungry, but the old man offered us nothing to eat. He sold us some gas and we left as soon as the storm began to let up. The highway was still closed and we saw no traffic until we reached Casper. After a few hours, the snow-plows came down from the north and we drove home. We were late for Christmas, but oh so happy to be back in Montana. After our freshman year ended, Jackie and I decided we'd had enough of school in Colorado. We were homesick and wanted to go to college at Montana State University. We wanted to go back where "the men were men and the sheep were nervous."

While I was away at school, Mom had been exiled to the bowels of Los Angeles. Dad had married his secretary and Bud had moved to the ranch after getting his degree in entomology. From that day on he called me Bug. Dad had sold our pink house and moved to our cabin in Bear Canyon. Howie had joined the Army and, to Dad's delight, was shipped overseas. Dad paid Jackie's mother to let me live with them in town. Jackie had two sisters, one was born blind and was remarkable in all aspects. I loved Jackie's mother, her sisters, and the tiny, two-bedroom old house. Her dad had been a Naval office in World War II. Soon after returning home from military service, he drove to West Yellowstone, hit a moose on a hairpin curve and was killed.

Jackie and I attended Montana State College together and we attended some functions at the Pi Phi house. These sorority girls were nice and down to earth. Very seldom was a girl admitted to veterinary school and I knew I'd have to keep my grades up if I had any chance at all. In addition to the normal subjects, I took as many science classes as I could. Most, but definitely not all, of my social life was put on hold. After two years of pre-vet, I applied to veterinary schools in Colorado and Washington. I was declined and told it was rare to be accepted before either finishing all four years of pre-vet or having a Masters degree. In fact, only one woman had been accepted to either school in ten years. I applied again the next year and was told that I would probably be accepted if I could raise my grade in physics from a "D" to a "B". Having a total mental block about physics, I thought only a miracle could raise my grade. Scheduled for a dental appointment, to my life long dentist who used hypnosis for sedation, I requested that during the hypnosis he remove my mental block about physics. To my amazement I studied for the final exam for sixteen uninterrupted hours and received the highest grade in the class. My grade was raised to a "B" and I was accepted to veterinary college in Washington after only three years of pre-vet studies. I got the acceptance letter at Jackie's and my guardian angel and I did hand springs around her house!

During college in Montana, I spent my spare time at the ranch helping Bud and riding Hitan, Mike and a new horse Blossom. She was a pretty palomino mare that enjoyed doing the tricks I had taught her. Hitan had been turned out with twenty mares. His foals were beautiful. Time had not broken our bond. When he saw me coming, he'd always meet me half way. I'd swing up on his back and spend peaceful, wonderful hours with him. I'd joined the college rodeo team and was running sixteen-second barrels on him. It wasn't a super time, but it was adequate. The college had a great equine program with only twenty students being accepted into it. We each got an unhandled two-

Trick horse, Blossom

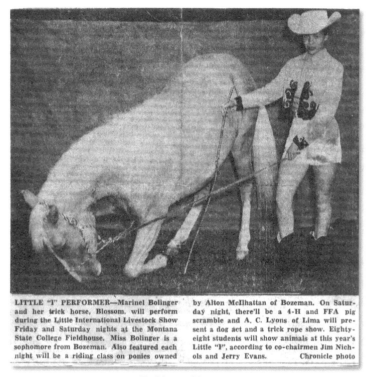

LITTLE "I" PERFORMER—Marinel Bolinger and her trick horse, Blossom, will perform during the Little International Livestock Show Friday and Saturday nights at the Montana State College Fieldhouse. Miss Bolinger is a sophomore from Bozeman. Also featured each night will be a riding class on ponies owned by Alton McIlhattan of Bozeman. On Saturday night, there'll be a 4-H and FFA pig scramble and A. C. Lyons of Lima will present a dog act and a trick rope show. Eighty-eight students will show animals at this year's Little "I", according to co-chairmen Jim Nichols and Jerry Evans. Chronicle photo

Trick horse, Blossom

year-old colt to train to be a quiet western pleasure horse and a hackamore reining horse. We took responsibilities for all those colts, including shoeing them. At the end of the semester, we showed our horses in the Little International Stock Show. I was asked to show my trick horses, Mike and Blossom. I dressed them up in Montana Pep Club sweaters and they rolled a keg of beer into the arena with their noses, sat down, drank a jug of beer, walked like they were drunk, and then fell over. The crowd loved them!

Jackie and I attended one more year of college together in Montana. That fall, I'd be a freshman at veterinary school and she would join the Peace Corps. A four-month hitchhiking trip through Europe would be a good sendoff. Three other girls joined us for part of the trip. We were on limited budgets. Mine was four hundred dollars for four months, including sea fare on an overloaded Italian ship. Hitchhiking was commonplace in Europe. We set out in our cut-off Levi's and sweatshirts. An extra pair was rolled up in our sleeping bags. Our nights were spent sleeping in the brush in our mummy bags. Hitch hiking, made it easy to get from one country to the next, as we explored twelve countries before we ran out of money. We stretched our money as far as we could, making a loaf of bread and cheese go a long way. As money ran out, we began eating food off of plates left by customers at cafes. While in Ireland, Jackie and I walked by the window of a small café. There was a plate of food that had hardly been touched. Seated by a stair-way, we quickly began to devour the deserted food. Screaming at us in a Northern Irish dialect, a large woman ran down the stairs hitting us with her purse. She had only gone to the restroom. The police were called as we ran out of the building and into a green field. " Run Jackie run," I yelled as we escaped into the country-side. Jackie and I left Ireland on a ferry-boat. It had three levels, for three classes of society. Just like in the movie "The Titanic" we rode the bottom level with the bottom class, sitting on gunny-sacks. Jackie, being Irish, knew the words to all the old classical Irish songs, as did I. We drank dark beer and sang along with the Irish poor. We knew the words better than they. We danced the Irish gig with our new friends and shared stories through out the night. I was glad I had kissed the Blarney stone!

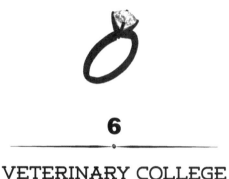

6

VETERINARY COLLEGE

Veterinary College was demanding and I was one of two females in a class of fifty. My classmates treated me well, except for four rebellious guys who spent most of their time trying to convince me I didn't belong. They delighted in sitting behind me, creating their own musical renditions with burps, belches and other obscene noises. At times, smells resembling sulfur gas would fill the air. They'd laugh so hard, that one fell out of his chair.

There was just one problem. I would laugh too and I'd be the one chastised for disturbing the class.

Anatomy class consisted of lectures and labs. All the animals we dissected were preserved in formaldehyde with their arteries dyed red, their veins blue. For our first-semester assignment, students were paired up and each pair got a dog and a cat to dissect. Dissection was long and tedious. Lab tests were difficult. There was no question, if you passed this course, you knew these two species inside and out! We formed teams of four and moved up to horses and cows for the second semester. The preserved horses and cows hung from the ceiling in a large circle. Lifelike in appearance, it was startling at first sight. The smell of formaldehyde was nearly overwhelming but I got used to it. I'm not sure the girls in my dormitory ever did, as my body reeked as I daily passed through the halls of the stately colonial-style building.

Spring came and most of our horses and cows had been dissected into small parts. One nice, warm day, the teacher announced we needed to discard whatever was left of our specimens because we'd be focusing on poultry dissection the last two weeks. A member of the "fabulous four" asked if I'd help him by carrying what remained of his cow's leg to the dump area out back. He placed the dissected leg in my arms. It was heavy and I had to cradle it close to my body it to keep from dropping it. As I neared the backroom, I felt something crawling up my neck and down my arms. I discovered the leg was infested with maggots! I hurled it ten feet across the room and frantically tried to brush off the hundreds of maggots crawling through my clothes and hair. Those guys rolled in laughter as I nearly lost my lunch. To this day, I still have difficulty in treating animals for maggot infestation. Secretly, I swore revenge. It came sooner than I'd expected. During the chicken dissection, I found my two hens were full of eggs. I removed the eggs and hid them in my lap. When the teacher left the room, I hurled eggs at my tormentors' heads and faces. What pleasure it was to see yolk dripping down their heads, into their eyes. The other classmates applauded and looked for eggs inside their chickens. Soon it was a free-for-all as the "war of eggs" got into full swing. Suddenly the room was silent. Two instructors were watching the battle. The "fabulous four" were reprimanded for their bad behavior and made to stay after class to clean up the mess. I laughed all the way down the corridor and into the warm sunshine. I'd survived the most difficult year of vet school—the freshman year.

The next three years went easier and, scholastically speaking, were more interesting. I'd married my beau from Montana and had a daughter and son during that time. Combining motherhood, housekeeping and school often overwhelmed me, sometimes to near exhaustion. I became the world's best cat-napper. We had eight hours of classes a day with ten-minute breaks in-between. The cot in the ladies restroom was my salvation. Five-to eight-minute naps between classes made up for hours of tending to babies throughout the night. When the bell rang, I'd rush to class, the telltale signs of sleep across my face. Classes after lunch were the hardest, as a full stomach required all the blood flow my brain needed. I could fake it for a short time, resting my head in my hand while my elbow locked onto the desk, but, eventually, the elbow gave way and my head would drop down with a thud. The "fabulous four" delighted in watching this, provided they weren't asleep as well. This was not a problem in all my classes, Dr. "Snow Job" was so good looking that sleep was out of the question, I was too intimidated by "The King" that my own adrenaline overrode any need to sleep, and my best professor kept us all captivated with his powerful voice and slides of poisonous plants, their height measured by beer cans. Other instructors didn't get such high marks. "Booger Bill" picked his nose while pacing back and forth. "Wormy," who taught parasitology, often was asleep at his desk before each class and, when he moved or spoke, it was so slow that we all napped during that class. "Turkey Lurky" and "Chicken Little" tried to teach poultry classes, but only got our attention when they wrung some poor, defenseless chicken's neck in sheer delight. Then we'd have to dissect the pile of bones and feathers to determine the cause of death, other than the fact its head was missing!

Junior and senior years consisted of morning lectures and afternoon clinics. We worked in small groups to diagnose and treat the caseloads at the animal hospital. We all wore the same brown coveralls. What a fashion statement I made between the seventh and ninth months of pregnancy in my brown coveralls. The guys named me "Nelly Jelly Belly," and our work went on. My body barely could furnish enough blood to nourish a baby and my brain. Fainting was not uncommon, but I considered it a disaster if it happened in the presence of my classmates. Sometimes my blood pressure failed me at the most awkward times. While taking the rectal temperature of a twelve-hundred-pound Holstein cow, I felt a little dizzy so I rested my head on her rump while proceeding with the task. The big farmer with red cheeks and bib overalls already had made it clear he was not sure a female should be examining his Bossy, especially a female who looked past term in pregnancy, as was Bossy. Farmer John stayed on the other side of the Holstein's rump to insure I was properly taking her temperature. My head began to swim. I prayed for more blood to flow, but it didn't come and the farmer looked in disbelief as I slipped down Bossys' hind legs and fell to the floor. The next thing I remembered was being lowered onto a cot in the ladies room by the obstetrics teacher. He seemed bewildered, but genuinely concerned, that one of his students had "hit the dust."

One instructor seemed to hate my being female. Of course, his morning lectures began at eight o'clock sharp. By the time I'd dressed and fed my baby girl, taken her to the babysitter, and driven twenty miles to school, often over icy roads, eight o'clock was long gone. The door to the room was closed and, if I tried to enter, I'd be reprimanded for my tardiness and told to stand in the hallway until his lecture was over. I also dreaded those weeks this instructor, who looked like an orangutan, would supervise my clinic rotation. While taking the temperature of a calf, my cantankerous thermometer darted from my fingers into the darkness of the calf's intestinal tract. I searched frantically for it but my fingers failed to reach it. Dr. Orangutan would be coming back soon to check on my work. Would this calf die of mercury poisoning or lacerated intestine? What should I do? Should I fake a temperature reading and write it on the chart and leave? The calf's big, soft brown eyes said "No." I ran to the small animal clinic and found the proctoscope. I hid it under a towel and raced back to the large animal clinic. Tying the calf to the corner of the stall, I got on all fours and inserted the scope into the rebellious calf. It was a battle to hold the calf still and an even tougher fight to see through the lens, which seemed to only show dark green matter. I couldn't give up now, even though my "Nelly Jelly Belly" was beginning to rebel against this physical endeavor. I heard a snicker, then a growly voice that only could be Dr. Orangutan's. "Did you lose something?" he asked. Then I heard howling laughter of the "fabulous four." This was a bad day; I wished I could climb through the scope and disappear from this life! The next day, the caretaker found the thermometer in the straw.

Rectally palpating cows and horses for pregnancy took hours of practice and was a major part of our education. During clinic rotation, several weeks were spent on ambulatory calls, where five students would accompany the instructor on his farm calls. Having been raised on a cattle ranch, I was anxious for my turn to go to a big ranch where we were to palpate hundreds of cows from early morning until late evening. The rancher and his hired hands were startled when I emerged from the veterinary ambulatory wagon. You could see their faces drop, did this mean they had to watch their vocabulary and limit their jokes? Little did they know that three years of veterinary school had made me immune to all forms of profanity and that I probably knew better jokes than they'd ever hear! I was third in line for pregnancy palpations and the last one in line before lunch at the ranch house. It was a fine spring day and I had just enjoyed a relaxing Easter break. After palpating about twenty-five cows in a row, my arm began to tire and all the cows' backsides were beginning to look alike. Only ten more cows until lunch, I thought. The palpations had gone smoothly and I began to feel confident about my decisions on the pregnancy status of each cow. Number twenty-six did not seem quite right. Was the fetus mummified and hard? Or was it an ovarian tumor? Compared to the other cows, nothing felt normal. I decided to clean her out real well and start over. Oh no. It felt like her ovaries were coming out with my hand. What the . . .! Out came colored Easter eggs. Everyone roared with laughter. The bovine Easter bunny was actually a bull the hired hands had stuffed with colored eggs while he was in the chute, behind me. The bull and I were the hit of the day!

During senior year, I decided that if I had the opportunity, I would specialize in equine medicine with emphasis on surgery and reproduction. I took every opportunity to palpate the horses provided for us in the large animal clinic. One afternoon I went early to the clinic in order to be the first to palpate the mares. I led the three patient old mares into the stocks and tied their heads. The pharmacy was not yet open, so I couldn't get any shoulder-length OB gloves. In fact, I didn't have any gloves to wear. My wedding ring was a half-carat marquise diamond and I always was careful to remove it before hand because its shape might harm the animal. But that day I hurried before the instructor and the rest of class arrived. The mares had been eating spring grass and were easy to clean out before I tried to ascertain their pregnancy status. Not having gloves didn't concern me. I always liked the smell of cow and horse manure. It made me a little homesick for the ranch. I decided the first mare was sixty days pregnant. The second was not pregnant and the third mare had a large fetus, heavy enough to drop over the pelvic brim, so I guessed she was probably five or six months pregnant. All was going smoothly until I went to wash up. My ring was gone! Which mare had my ring inside her? I raced back to the mares and started my search: Mare number 1, no ring; Mare number 2, no ring; same for Mare number 3. I searched through all their droppings. No ring. Dr. Orangutan and four classmates entered the room. "You're early for a change," he snorted. "At least we don't have to catch the mares. They're ready for us." "Not only that," said a classmate, "they're already cleaned out. This should be easy."

Dr. Orangutan then palpated all three mares to check their pregnancies before turning them over to his students. As each student palpated, I held my breath. They threw the remaining manure on the floor and, as each horse apple was flung, I raced to examine it. "Are you hungry?" growled Dr. Orangutan. "Oh no," I replied. "I'm just trying to find worms for my parasite collection." As each student palpated the mares, I became more anxious. Madly ripping horse apples apart. "Finding any worm?" the professor asked. "No sir. No parasites." Finally, it was my turn and my last chance to find my beautiful ring. I palpated each mare as deeply and carefully as possible. Dr. Orangutan became impatient. "Well, are they pregnant or what?" he angrily asked. I gave him the correct answer for each and he grumbled about how slow I was. At five o'clock, he ordered us to turn the mares out and clean up the mess. To everyone's delight, I volunteered to do it myself. Now I was alone with the mares and the waiting game began. I called the babysitter, told her there was an emergency and I might be late. The mares had been cleaned out so well, it seemed like hours before they began producing more horse apples. They were hungry and getting fidgety. The old paint rolled her blue eyes as if to say, "If you'd leave, we could go to pasture." Two hours went by. I was ready to give up when the old paint mare groaned, rolled those big blue eyes, and passed a few more apples. This time, there was something hard in one. It was my ring. It looked more like an emerald, but I didn't care. I was exhausted as I cleaned my hands and arms, and returned the shine to my ring. I backed the mares out of the stocks and led them to pasture. The old paint mare snorted and bolted away in sheer delight, as if she knew we shared a very deep secret.

Being pregnant was becoming more and more difficult. "Very heavy in foal," remarked my classmates. The brown suit was getting tighter and tighter and "Nelly Jelly Belly" was the only name I heard. The timing for this pregnancy was not well planned. It was the first semester of my senior year and meat inspection lab lasted two weeks. All federally regulated meat processing plants require a veterinarian's inspection for humane kill and to examine the meat meant for human consumption. I was dreading this class but, for the next two weeks, I'd have to watch cattle and pigs being slaughtered if I wanted to graduate.

I was due to foal at any time and felt twelve months pregnant! Class was to meet the meat inspector at the slaughter plant's entrance, then proceed to the kill floor on the fifth floor. Even on the outside, the old brick building reeked with an offensive odor. My class was nowhere to be found. The first two doors I tried were locked. The third door opened into a dark, dirty hallway that led to a box car-type of elevator. It creaked as I ascended floor after floor. It stopped in front of a rusty door. With difficulty, I opened the old metal door. As I stepped forward, a massive form swung past my head. Thick, oozing fluid covered my body. "Get the hell out of there," someone yelled. I was green from vomit the executed cow had showered me with as it swung past me on a trolley holding its hind legs! This was my introduction to the dreaded kill floor!

I'd nearly become a statistic and, at that moment, felt like it would've been a blessing. Except for my four tormentors, who could not control their laughter, the class was divided between those who said I'd made their day and those who realized I'd nearly been killed. The men on the kill floor stopped and stared in wonder. I was probably the first female they'd seen on the kill floor, not to mention term pregnant and covered in vomit!

The remaining two weeks at the slaughter plant were long and I was miserable.

Happily returning from my clinic rotation at the slaughterhouse, my husband, baby girl, Hallie and our modest house trailer nestled, in the wheat field, were a welcomed sight. As I had been gone for two weeks, the toilet seat had, for most of the time been left elevated. Unknown to me a visitor from the barn, Senor El Raton, had been enjoying his "night cap" from the toilet bowl. Much to his surprise, he could not retreat from the water once the seat was set down. Being nine months pregnant, frequent trips to the bathroom were necessary. Sitting upon the throne, I remembered the horrors of the slaughterhouse. Something was tickling my butt. Maybe I was going into labor? No it wasn't cramps, just tickling. Arising from the throne, I switched on the light. Large, brown and furry, with big liquid brown eyes, and very long whiskers, was a rat. I think he just tickled my fancy. I couldn't let him drown. He only wanted a drink of water. No choice, but to wake my husband. "There's a rat in the toilet and I want to put him outside. Please help me," I pleaded. "There is a what in the what?" he replied half asleep. After repeating myself, husband sleepily followed me to the bathroom. Seeing Mr. Raton he grabbed his gun. After all, he had shot mice and rats off the walls in the first old farm-house we had occupied. " No, no," I begged, he's just thirsty. Lets chase him out the back door so he can go to the barn, he won't be back again." We lifted the toilet seat, blocked the hallway and Mr. Rat disappeared into the night.

So tired, I fell into a deep sleep. Soft and wispy, something was stroking my cheek. I guess my husband really did miss me while I was gone for the last two weeks. Rolling over, I was face to face with Mr. Raton, those soft brown eyes. "Three is a crowd," I said, as I whisked him off my pillow. Back to a beautiful sleep, where I could smell the pines and hear a babbling brook. Dropping my arm off the bed I felt the water. Had my water broke? No, the water was deep on the bedroom floor. Again I woke my poor husband. "The trailer is flooding, and it's not even raining. "The what is what?" he yelled as he leaped out of bed into knee deep water. "Your little brown furry friend, you know the one who wouldn't come back again has chewed the water line to the washing machine in half. Most of our trailer is under water!"

Buck naked, he grabbed a weapon from the closet, clawing through the water in pursuit of the terrified, but fast swimming rat. Up and down the hall they went, even into the kitchen and back again. "No, no, I screamed, open the side door and the rat and water will spill out side." Nothing is more determined than a husband whose wife has crossed the line. He was bottoms up and belly deep in the water, as he raced after the rat on his hands and knees. He repeatedly swung the steel rod at the terrified little rodent. Suddenly I heard him yell "Geronimo." Blood and guts splattered on the hallway walls as the clock struck twelve. The little bird emerged twelve times from the cuckoo clock, as the rat lay dying on my husbands submersed back!

Mid-term exams were approaching. I felt so big, I considered using the calf puller to get into my brown coveralls. The instructor for large animal clinics had made it clear all semester that he did not approve of graduating a woman into his field of veterinary medicine. One failure meant permanent dismissal with no chance to make up the grade. This instructor, Dr. Orangutan, who had taught the eight o'clock lectures, and large animal clinics, also taught large animal restraint. He knew I'd have trouble restraining the heavy ewes by lifting them up and setting them on their haunches. I weighed one hundred fifteen pounds pregnant and most of the ewes weighed two hundred pounds or more. It was nearly impossible to lift them past my "Nelly Jelly Belly." I knew he was laying for me and I was ready. I remembered what Dad had always told me, "when the going gets tough, the tough get going!"

Each of us had to perform three restraint maneuvers. I was to twitch a horse, catch and restrain a calf and restrain a sheep. I knew the clinic horse. He was a ringer. He'd probably been born a bronco or eaten Loco Weed. He had one eye removed in Junior Surgery class and had no use for humans. His one good eye saw only red! I approached him slowly as he had a reputation for rearing and striking. I hoped he liked women better than men. I needed every advantage I could get! I petted him on his good side so he could see me. I knew that, when I reached for his nose with the chain twitch, he'd go crazy, so I went soft and slow. He relaxed for a moment as I kept petting him, moving down to his soft muzzle. Then I grabbed it with all my might. He backed and reared. I hung on like a leach slipping the chain over his muzzle and twisting the handle

Me-Ewe

hard enough so it wouldn't slip, but not so tight that he'd continue to fight me. He lowered his head and closed his good eye in submission. I petted him in praise, wishing he could go to pasture for the rest of his life.

Catching the calf in its pen and inserting the bolus with a bolus gun was uneventful, as I'd tied more calves than I could remember for the rodeo team. Next came the big test, lifting the two-hundred-pound ewe I'd not been able to lift all semester. By this time, I had such an adrenaline surge that I felt I could lift a mountain! I was mad and I wasn't going to be beat. I approached the ewe from the back, grabbed a handful of wool from each side and gave it all I had. She lifted so high off the ground that I had two handfuls of wool as I sat her hindquarters down between my feet. She sat quietly, resting against my abdomen. Dr. Orangutan was not happy, but even the "fabulous four" seemed delighted at my victory. "Bet you can't put a bolus down her," the professor growled, handing me the huge pill and balling gun. I opened her mouth, inserted the balling gun down her esophagus, halfway to her heart, and discharged the bolus. "She's going to cough it up," he said over and over. He was wrong and that was the last performance I had to make for Dr. Orangutan.

The next day I was scheduled to take my last exam, for small animal medicine. The test seemed easy and I finished before the rest of the class. It was a Friday and I was relieved it was over. I was tired and had some abdominal pain. That evening, I gave birth to a large, healthy baby boy— Willie! I slept for most of that weekend but dragged myself to my eight o'clock class Monday morning. Neither pregnancy nor child birth were considered an excuse from attendance. I sat on a pillow and hoped for a fire so class would end early! That afternoon, our test scores were posted. When Dr. Snow Job returned our tests, he turned to the class and said, "Nelly got the highest grade in the class. That shows that two heads are better than one. Congratulations, Nelly. Are you pregnant again so you can continue to get good grades?"

Graduation day was finally here, a beautiful, sunny day, with my family in attendance. Dad came over from Montana and presented me with a black leather doctors' bag. As we threw our graduation caps into the air, we were pronounced Doctors of Veterinary Medicine!

7

STARTING PRACTICE ON
A SHOE STRING

As my husband had steady employment in the area where the vet school was, I had no chance of beginning my career in a group practice as no veterinarian would face the financial risk of setting up a clinic with the veterinary college right there. So, immediately after graduation, I opened up our trailer house as my first clinic. The portable dishwasher was the surgery table and the bathtub was the post-op recovery area. I also equipped my pickup truck with a toolbox to carry vet supplies for ambulatory services.

To my delight, I started building a practice with a list of clients. Mostly they were friends or friends of friends, but clients nonetheless. My three-year-old daughter, Hallie, was designated "assistant surgeon." Luckily, Willie couldn't walk yet. My first surgery was for a dog with persistent neck pain. I'd taken advance small animal surgery and performed a cervical disk fenestration in class and, although my setting was primitive, I felt my skills were adequate. The surgery was a success. Two weeks later, the owner's daughter brought the dog in to have its stitches removed. I asked her to hold the black cocker on the dishwasher as I began suture removal. She bent her six-foot, frame over the counter and, although there was no blood exposed during the suture removal, she fainted. Her long body slid down the kitchen wall, her feet kicked the dishwasher, propelling it and the startled dog through the kitchen, and into the living room. The dog was still astride that dishwasher when it hit the hallway entrance! The girl's white and clammy body stretched quietly on the floor. After rescuing the howling dog, I revived the girl and her father came and took both medical cases home.

My first house call was to castrate a bull calf. The charge at the veterinary college was three dollars, so I quoted the caller five. Following his directions, the twenty-mile drive ended in a wooded area at an old cabin. An old man emerged. "Where's the calf, sir?" I asked. "I've come to castrate it." He was a crippled old logger and a man of few words. "Up yonder," he said, pointing to a pine-covered mountain. I grabbed my ropes and emasculators and followed him up the mountain. "Over yonder, he is," the man said. "Might be hard to catch but sometimes he eats grain from this bucket." Sure enough, the six-hundred-pound calf came to the bucket and let the man slip a rope around his neck. We tied the neck rope to a pine tree and the calf bellowed in protest. I'd only castrated small calves with two men on them or with the calf inside a chute. My only choice was to rope the hind legs and dalley the rope to another tree. I was happy to be physically fit, as stretching the calf tightly between two trees was not a simple process. The old man put his knee in the calf's neck and I proceeded to castrate the bewildered animal as quickly as possible. Untied, the calf rolled the whites of his eyes and bellowed. He staggered for his footing and disappeared into the forest. As we walked back to the cabin, I wondered if this was what large animal medicine was all about. The old logger retrieved a five-dollar bill from under his mattress and offered me a home-made cookie. "Sometimes Molly, my horse, comes inside to eat cookies." Indeed she did, and the three of us shared the warm oatmeal treats.

The call obviously had cost me more than five dollars in gas, but the logger and his horse Molly had made the trip worthwhile. I'd always respected and admired loggers and sheepherders. Maybe it was part of my Montana heritage.

The pines were cool and the mountain majestic. I did not begrudge the call. I did, however, learn to ask "how far?" and "how big?" before quoting a price.

Willie was nearly a year old and it became more apparent that the in-utero influence of the "fabulous four" from vet school days was not to be taken lightly. He happily survived on a few hours sleep and, before seven months of age, held the track record for crawling. His favorite pastime was not playing with his many toys, but rather eating downer flies and sticking hairpins in electrical outlets. Nothing seemed out of his busy reach. His big blue eyes followed my every move. He thrived on the clients who brought their animals to the trailer. He loved to see kitty come for surgery, but this got out of hand when he began biting the tails of the cats as they hung over the dishwasher while being spayed.

Cats waiting for surgery

A Palouse Profile

Youthful Lady Veterinarian
Designs, Runs Alpine Clinic

8

FINALLY, MY OWN HOSPITAL

It was time to build a real clinic with an apartment above it where we could reside. To my surprise, the dean of the veterinary college helped me get a loan from the bank. He felt that a private practice was needed in the area. Finally I had my own veterinary clinic, a beautiful A-frame with large windows in the front. It contained: reception, examination, surgery, recovery, isolation, and boarding rooms. We lived in an apartment above the hospital.

Anxiously, I awaited my first patient. Through the large glass front of the A-frame building, I could see a car pull off the main highway, cross the wooden bridge and stop in front of the clinic. A woman and her daughter emerged from the car, carrying something in a small blanket. I hoped it was a kitten or puppy, coming for its first exam and vaccination. That would be a wonderful way to get the clinic off to a good start and begin building up a good client relationship. They burst through the front door, blurting out that their pet mouse was sick. We never learned to treat mice in vet school as my school never taught classes for the care of pocket pets.

I only knew that Oliver, my pet owl, ate the white mice from the veterinary research department. Unfolded, the blanket revealed a small, emaciated, brown rodent with glazed-over, beady eyes. It lay panting on its side and looked older than any mouse I'd ever seen. The woman described how it had been captured in their house five years ago and now was part of the family. "Doctor, do something," she demanded. I began a shotgun treatment for possible infection and shock, injecting a tiny dose of penicillin and steroids into the small creature. The mouse began to tremble. Its legs went stiff and it rolled up, staring at me. I began mouth-to-mouse resuscitation for several minutes as the patient's respiration ceased. I could still feel its heart beating, but not as fast as mine! When the heart stopped beating, I laid the mouse on its blanket and informed the woman that her pet was dead. The daughter began sobbing uncontrollably. The woman yelled that I was the worst mouse doctor she'd ever met, grabbed the blanket and bolted out the door. My confidence had been shaken. My first client, in my new hospital, despised me and my first patient had died despite my heroic efforts.

Subsequent days brought new clients with normal problems and my confidence gradually was restored. The veterinary college stopped boarding dogs and my boarding facility, which housed dogs and cats, was usually full. This increased the number of animals for vaccinations, grooming, surgery and other medical problems. Boarding was not my idea of veterinary medicine and, although it brought in clients, it also caused several cases of near cardiac arrest for me.

The dog kennels were nice with heated floors and large outdoor cyclone fence runs. Answering the phone one day, my favorite teacher from vet school asked if I'd board their house guests' sheltie for two weeks. They came with the dog, its bed and several toys. The woman was nervous and thin, he quite fat and quiet; they fussed over their dog for twenty minutes before leaving him in my care. We lived above the clinic so I didn't worry about vandalism or theft. The sheltie appeared happy in its bed with its toys. All seemed fine when I did my ten p.m. rounds of the clinic. Morning came early. Boarders had to be fed and the place cleaned before the clinic opened at eight o'clock. Being a recent graduate, I couldn't afford kennel help or a receptionist. I did it all myself. It was during the morning feeding I discovered the Sheltie missing. That clever little dog must've scaled the nine-foot cyclone fence like a monkey. I called the owners. She answered, began wailing and slammed down the phone. They soon showed up at the clinic, along with my favorite instructor. This was their only child and they became hysterical.

Within two hours, eight bloodhounds and their handler arrived from Idaho. The hounds sniffed the shelties bed, blanket and toys, bayed, set their noses to the ground and set off to the east, towards Idaho. In hot pursuit behind the hounds were the two visitors, she in a thin summer dress, he drenched in sweat as he ran as fast as his obesity allowed. The dogs zigzagged back and forth, across a shallow creek, the railroad tracks, the highway, and finally into wheat fields that spanned the distance to the state line. I jumped bareback upon my horse, trying to follow the procession, but was soon cut off by fences with no gates. The party returned, empty-handed, several hours later. This procedure was repeated for several days and each time, the hounds took a new route. On the fifth day, the hounds were called off and the owners gave up in despair. I managed to get little work done and managed even less

Newspaper clipping from
March 6, 1957

sleep. On the ninth day of the sheltie's disappearance, I was staring aimlessly out the clinic's front door. Down the railroad tracks, from the direction opposite the intense search, walked the sheltie. He crossed the wooden bridge and scratched on the clinic door to be let in. He seemed to be none the worse for wear and was happy to see me. I was so happy to see him! I placed him in maximum security with his possessions and called his family who were planning to return home to California that day. It was a joyful reunion. To insure that such an incident was not repeated, I reinforced the run area with a ten-foot-high block wall beyond the nine-foot cyclone fence.

Then there was Mike the mina bird. The bird's owner wanted to spend the summer in Europe so Mike came to board for three months. I was familiar with mina birds as my family had one in Montana that was a delight. He had a great vocabulary and could sing cowboy songs! I hoped that Oliver the owl would like another bird in the room with him.

Oliver proved to be a female and was a delight to everyone. Given to me by a client who found her near the road, she still had her baby fluff, and was small and cuddly. Growing up with us in our upstairs apartment. She had free run of the house and after learning to fly, with her six-foot wing-span, she had to tilt sideways to fly down the halls. Her silent flights surprised guests, especially when she landed on their heads. My intent was to turn her back to the wild but she refused to leave, circling outside the clinic, she would reappear at the door, seeming quite pleased to be a house owl. After being shot at twice by boys walking the railroad tracks, we decided to build a floor-to-ceiling cage with a large tree limb and flagstone background inside the clinic reception room. She usually sat with her back to the reception desk. When a client came in, her head would turn one hundred eighty degrees to inspect the visitor. She was fond and fearless of people and their dogs. She loved cats. To her, cats were meant to eat. Twice, while flying around the apartment, Oliver made silent advances on the litter of kittens we raised. Once, she grabbed the leg of a client's cat that had jumped off its' owners lap to stalk the big owl. After a brief tug of war, the cat was retrieved with only minor scratches. Although Oliver showed no fear of dogs, no matter how large, she had a great respect for Cricket the coyote. When Cricket wandered past her cage, Oliver would fluff up her feathers to double her size, spread

Oliver the owl

her wings to their complete width and snap her beak between her two large, round, yellow eyes. She ruffled her feathers when a woman in a full-length red fox fur coat came to the clinic. The owl exhibited her threatening behavior, much like she did to Cricket. The woman in the fur coat grabbed her poodle from my arms and made a quick exit.

The veterinary research department provided Oliver with white mice. They delivered these frozen mice to my hospital. As I was finishing up a surgery, my assistant advised me she had to leave for a short time. "By the way, the veterinary school just dropped off some mice for Oliver. They told me to put them in the freezer so I did, but they are alive" she exclaimed as she walked out the door. I couldn't believe my ears. They're alive and in the freezer. I thought the research department humanely put the mice to sleep with an anesthetic gas before freezing them. Completing the surgery was difficult as I was having trouble concentrating while thinking about the mice. Finally the surgery was done and the patient carefully placed in a warm recovery area. Opening the freezer revealed about two hundred little white mice staring at me with pink frightened eyes as they huddled together in the back of the freezer. Collecting them, I took them to the grooming area, placed them in warm water then dried them with the hair dryer. I couldn't feed them alive to my owl, so I turned them loose in a large wheat field. Apparently, they fared well as white mice are still see in the surrounding country-side.

Cricket was a wonderful coyote. She had been plowed out of her den before her eyes were open and was the third coyote I'd raised on a bottle. She was highly intelligent and won top honors in obedience school. She had free run in and out of the clinic and particularly liked women and children. Her best friend was Shannon, our Irish setter, and she got along well with the family cats. Cricket would follow me when I rode horse back and played in the snow with the children. Together, they dug great snow tunnels to explore. Cricket paid little attention to Oliver the owl. When Mike the mina bird arrived in his large cage, he was placed near Oliver who was fascinated, but Mike wasn't that interested in the owl. We were anxious to hear Mike talk, but his vocabulary was limited. Besides eating, he would sit on his perch and scream in a high-pitched note that would wake the dead! No one could stand being in the same room with him; the sound vibrated off the flagstone wall. This irritated Oliver. Then the clients got annoyed, so Mike spent the rest of his stay in the back room. Six weeks of summer passed and Mike hadn't stopped screaming the whole time except for when he was covered at night. Cricket was good to keep her distance from his cage, but never lost her keen interest in the noisy visitor. One day, while treating a patient, I heard a scream that made my blood run cold. I dashed to the back room. Mike's headless body sat on the perch, his wings still flapping. Cricket gave me a look of guilt, as she swallowed his head, beak and all! How do you tell a client your coyote ate her bird's head? She returned home six weeks after the incident. All I could do was to tell her the truth. I waited, expecting to be threatened with a lawsuit by a hysterical woman. She didn't speak for a long time. "My dear, this indeed is an unusual circumstance," she said at last. "It's obvious that it's caused you considerable anxiety." She went on to describe how a friend had given the bird to her and she felt obligated to keep him even though his screaming was a constant annoyance. "Mike will not be missed by me, I assure you," she said, describing how she'd wanted him put to sleep several times but never could go through with it. "It appears Cricket executed the plan very efficiently, and I doubt that Mike never knew what was coming."

Gradually my clientele grew; there didn't seem to be enough hours in the day. I was glad to have taken advanced surgery courses as this gave me the confidence I needed to operate on whatever problem came through the door. I hired a well-trained assistant, and Karen and I became a good team. Excellent with both patients and their owners, Karen had a good sense of humor, making the long, hard days pleasant. We were the first private clinic to detect salmon poisoning in dogs that ate that fish, we performed complicated orthopedic procedures, and we even de-scented a skunk or two. The last skunk I de-scented definitely was the last I'd ever do. The surgery requires the animal's scent glands be carefully dissected and removed. There's always the chance that a scent gland could break open during the operation, and it happened with that last skunk. The smell was horrific. I tried not to breathe. My eyes watered so much I could barely see, but I had to finish the procedure, now twice as difficult as the deflated gland would be extremely hard to isolate and dissect from the surrounding tissue. My full waiting room emptied before I finished removing the gland. With her hand over her mouth and her eyes blinking through the tears, Karen said if I ever de-scented another skunk, she'd quit! We burst into laughter, which only made me inhale more of the pungent air. Half an hour later, I ran coughing and gagging out of surgery, thankful it was over!

Although my main interest was to specialize in equine medicine and surgery, there were few horses in the area, as wheat fields occupied most of the land, not pastures. Two of my first ambulatory horse calls were memorable ones. As a vet student, I'd gone to the president of the University of Idaho' home several times before to treat his horses. I was surprised when he called my newly opened clinic and asked if I'd vaccinate his horses for sleeping sickness and tetanus. This would be an easy, routine call, I thought as I gathered my vaccinations, alcohol and cotton in a bucket and followed the president to the stables. He was a tall, handsome and pleasant man and I felt comfortable being there. I gave the tetanus shot first. The big bay hunter didn't seem to notice. "This is a cinch," I thought. Next came the sleeping sickness shot, which was to go into the skin of the neck, not the muscle. Completing the task, I patted the horse and turned to the owner. Droplets of vaccine were running off his glasses! I'd pushed the needle through both layers of skin and let vaccine fly right into the president's face. He wiped his glasses off with his shirttail. I ran to my truck for another dose of vaccine, that I administered carefully, under his now watchful eye. Gently he said, "we only learn by our mistakes. I hope you will continue to be my veterinarian."

There was only one large horse stable in the area. I'd been there many times on ambulatory calls while still in school. The owner had a string of show horses plus twenty boarding horses. He wanted me to treat a large swelling on a horse's chest that had developed after the horses' owner had administered a vaccination. The timing for this call was bad. My babysitter hadn't shown up that morning and I was tending to Willie on my own. He was at the "fast scramble" stage and could walk if he had furniture or a hand to hang onto. Extremely active, he'd crawl with his Playtex baby bottle, empty or full, in his mouth. His favorite word was "truck." I bundled him up, grabbed his bottle and put him in his car seat in the truck. His big, round blue eyes showed his delight as we sped down the back roads. He wiggled and squirmed, his bottle swinging from his mouth, but he knew it was wrong to get out of his seat without me helping. We arrived and I put the truck in park, set the emergency brake, and strapped Willie into his car seat. I walked down the steep hill to the recently remodeled horse show barn, which was the envy of horsemen throughout the area.

The horse owner led me to the new wing where the big, roan Tennessee walking mare turned to face me. An abscess the size of a basketball protruded from her chest. She was running a temperature and wasn't eating. The owner explained she had given her horse a shot three days ago and the lump appeared soon after that, increasing in size each day. I opened the black medical bag Dad gave me for graduation and clipped and scrubbed the area with soap and alcohol. Scalpel in hand, I asked the woman to step back as the abscess might drain some. Suddenly there was a loud crash. The barn shook and the mare jumped forward, into my scalpel blade. The blade went deep, cutting several inches into the abscess. Purulent exudate shot out, covering the nervous owner, several bystanders and me. The foul-smelling pus looked like red-flecked cream of mushroom soup; the audience scattered and I was left, bewildered. "What was that? Was it a sonic boom or an earthquake?" I headed toward the sound of the crash and there, two stalls down, was my truck. Willie was at the steering wheel, his bottle swinging from his mouth. "Truck. Truck, Mommy!" he yelled, dropping his bottle and scrambling back into his car seat. Once again, my guardian angel had been tested and passed with flying colors: The stall my truck crashed into was the only one that didn't contain a horse. Willie wasn't injured. In fact, he seemed to be enjoying the moment, and the mare quickly healed.

Willie became increasingly more active. A play-pen could not contain his athletic ability. At times, I had no choice but to put him in a big stainless-steel cage next to surgery, where he could watch me and I could watch him. He played with his toys and his precious bottle. To this day Willie tells any one who will listen, that his mother raised him in a dog cage. Hallie, now five, was a great assistant, as she loved to wear her doctor's smock and help run the clinic. Willie took three more turns at driving. He was a mechanical genius and, when determined, could easily shift the pickup into neutral and release the emergency brake. He knew the exact procedure. One time, I left him squirming in his infant seat while I removed groceries from the back of our station wagon. I took my eye off him long enough to bend over and pick up spilled apples. The car began rolling backward, almost knocking me flat! Somehow I regained my balance, crawled through the back of the station wagon, into the front seat, and pulled Willie from the steering wheel as I slammed on the brakes. He repeated this maneuver in a busy parking lot, only this time he turned the radio volume on full blast so every one within a block could see a frantic mother scramble to stop her runaway vehicle. "It was time for a vacation. I packed up the kids as we prepared to go to see their grandparents. Hallie, all dressed up to see Grandmother, sat patiently while I loaded Willie into his seat. As soon as I sat behind the wheel, the telephone rang. First I ignored it, but went inside after it wouldn't stop ringing. Before I had a chance to hang up, Hallie came through the door; her new dress filthy and full of cockle burrs. "I'm not going to see Grandmother if Willie is driving," she sobbed. "If Willie is what!" I exclaimed. "He's a careless driver," she said. "I'm staying home." I looked out the window. The station wagon was out in the field. It had rolled backwards down the hill, turned off the road, backed through a barbed-wire fence and stopped just short of the barn. Willie was behind the wheel, his bottle swinging back and forth, as he tried to steer.

After a week's vacation, I was ready to return home and resume work. I'd missed Cricket, Shannon, Oliver and, the newest addition that the Easter Bunny had brought Heidi the goat. Heidi, bottle-raised by Hallie and Willie, was certain she was human. She was a large Alpine goat, with a liver-brown coat, long curled horns and bright, yellow eyes. It was not my nature to cage my pets, except for Oliver, who had free run over the whole place after hospital hours. Heidi adored me and followed me everywhere she could. She'd affectionately rub her horns against the back of my legs. If I didn't pay her adequate attention, she'd throw her head up, butting me soundly until my attention was fully on her. She loved to rear up on her hind legs and dance. She'd do this on verbal command or whenever she wanted to intimidate someone. If that someone appeared frightened of her, she'd dance them into a corner, bow her head and raise her hackles in sheer delight. Clients knew Heidi and her antics well, as she loved to greet them at the door. She listened for the doorbell chime. When it rang, she would race madly from the back room and dance for anyone who entered. If a new client or their pet were frightened by a dancing goat, Karen or I would grab Heidi by her horns and pull her down the hall to the back room. Heidi objected to this treatment and, if possible, would run out the back door and begin dancing on the front porch or jump onto the client's car. She knew this was not acceptable behavior and delighted in it all the more. She'd jump from the hood to the top of the car and back down to the ground, never taking her eyes off the reception room. Sometimes the clients wouldn't accept her antics and she'd have to be captured and tied up, which was the worst punishment for her. Heidi loved to ride in any vehicle. If a client left a door open, she would jump inside, waiting for a ride. Some clients, being distracted by their pet, would not notice Heidie in the back seat until the saw her from their rear view mirror. This nearly caused several vehicular accidents. The A-framed clinic had a forty-foot cedar shake roof that Heidi would scale. There she would gleefully dance and show off to spectators on the ground. Another favorite pass-time was to jump on the horse shelters' metal roof and prance until the horses ran wildly into the field. When they returned to eat, she'd repeat her maneuver. Her favorite horse was our yearling stallion Hai Karatie. He enjoyed Heidi as a challenge and playmate. She'd race back and forth in his corral, as he worked her back and forth, like a cutting horse.

Heidi earned honor and respect the day the IRS man came to audit our books. Business had increased and bookkeeping was at least six month's behind as it was not my forte. It consisted of a card table in the spare office piled high with paper, next to a couple of paper-filled cardboard boxes. The IRS man was stern and unpleasant. He'd allotted three days to review my books. I led him into the room and pointed to the piles of paper and boxes. Karen and I looked at each other in despair; three days would be a long, long time. Heidi sensed our apprehension. She didn't like this stranger, either, and raised her hackles high as they could go. He sat down and went to work. I closed the door and Karen and I went to the back room to treat a patient. Hearing a banging noise, we went to the front of the clinic. Heidi was butting the office door with her horns. The door opened. Heidi reared up and danced toward the startled IRS auditor. Her hackles at full height as she leaped onto the table, jumping up and down on the piles of papers. She lowered her neck and threatened the man. He backed up in the chair, which pleased her and, in triumph, she passed wind and left a few "raisins" on the table. She then jumped through the air, scattering all the papers, as she raced out the door. Next, she jumped on the hood of the government vehicle, dancing back and forth over the length of the car, her eyes staring at the man on the other side of the big glass window. All composure left the auditor. He grabbed his briefcase and muttered, "Anyone who lives in this zoo couldn't possibly be dishonest!"

Conner was nice, but why did my husband tell him he could share my office with me? Just because we lived in the apartment above the hospital, he never missed his daily request for me to fix his lunch. I rarely took time to eat lunch myself. This was getting old.

A client owning several cats brought them in to board. "Please worm them while they are here. I'm sure they are full of tape worms, as they are such good mousers." He requested.

He was right, they produced a lot of tape worms after their medication. Karen and I looked at each other with a smirk on our faces. "There are at least three cups full of tape worms and they look just like pasta. Conner will soon be asking for lunch. Let's give him a meal he will always remember!" Carefully washing the worms we placed them on one of my nicer plates, topped them with marinade sauce and cheese, then added a little tossed salad. "Looks like a meal fit for a king," I exclaimed. Connor was happy to see us deliver his lunch. "Looks good," he said. " I always like Italian these noodles look great, thanks"

Dipping his fork into our special meal, he attempted his first bite. "Oh my God their moving, the noodles are moving!" Karen and I ran out of the room in uncontrollable laughter. Connor never bothered me for a meal again.

One aspect of having a clinic in competition with a veterinary college was that I knew my clients had faith in me and enjoyed coming to the clinic, or they wouldn't be here, especially since the college charged a lot less. Our loyal clients often would send us greeting cards and gifts. Two of the boarding dogs looked forward to their stays with us. Their owners would bring them in the front door and the dogs would go to the kennel room and scratch the door, wanting to be let in.

The wheat farming community of Pullman, Washington, was infested with enormous wharf rats that arrived via barges hauling wheat down the Columbia River to the Pacific Ocean. The rats would enter any open building, including our clinic. They found our kennel, filled with servings of dog and cat food, quite the convenience. There were too many to trap and, with all the domestic animals around, poisons couldn't be used. We decided to see what Oliver could do. We'd leave her in the kennel room after dark, but she'd only kill one or two a night. The rat problem continued to grow. It was solved when I received a present from a former instructor and friend, two large, black-footed ferrets. The day they arrived, I was busy in surgery so the friend left them in their cage in the back room. While I was closing surgery, Willie appeared, holding a huge rat by the tail. We wanted to test how effective ferrets were as rat-killers, so Willie dropped his catch into their cage. Each ferret instantly went for the rat's jugular vein. That rat was dead within seconds. We turned the beautiful ferrets loose behind the kennel and not one rat or ground squirrel was seen in the clinic area again.

Mrs. Edwards was a dear and definitely on our "preferred client" list. In her late fifties, she had a house full of dogs and cats she'd rescued from various fates. They were healthy and happy in her care. Alcohol was no stranger to her. It often was strong on her breath when she brought her pets to the clinic and, at times, she needed help getting back into her car but her kindness outweighed her addiction. There was only one door into our apartment above the clinic. A long flight of wooden stairs out side, opened directly into the master bedroom. One warm, summer night, around one-thirty in the morning, I heard steps coming up the stairs. The door flew open and my husband and I sat up to see Mrs. Edwards' teetering figure approaching. "Please Doctor, please save this poor cat I've run over. I'll feel so bad if it dies," said the staggering woman before she tossed the mass of fur into our bed and stumbled back down the stairs, into the night. I flipped on the light and examined the pile of gray striped fur. Still half asleep, my husband asked if I could save it. "I don't believe so, dear," I exclaimed. "Mrs. Edwards may have run over this poor cat tonight but someone else ran over it a week or so ago!" It was crawling with maggots, its flesh nearly gone. Both of us leaped out of bed, brushing maggots off our backs. I gathered the pancake-flat cat, the maggots and loose fur into the sheet and threw them out the door. We showered and spent the rest of the night in the guest room. As soon as the clinic opened, Mrs. Edwards called to ask if the cat was doing better. I could only tell her it had been injured beyond help.

Castrating horses was a common surgery. After administering a general anesthetic the surgery was usually performed on the lawn behind the hospital. Shannon our Irish-setter, was always the surgical assistant. She knew what lay ahead as I filled my bucket with disinfectant, emasculators and scalpel. On one such occasion, my husband came home just as I had anesthetized the horse and was beginning to perform the procedure. The adrenaline in the young horse began to over ride the anesthetic. It was attempting to get up before the procedure was completed. I convinced hubby to sit on the horse's neck as I quickly proceeded. Shannon sat near by, anxiously waiting. First testicle off, Shannon grabbed it midair, second testicle, she jumped up and retrieved it, also swallowing it whole. Hubby was unaware of this procedure and proceeded to loose his lunch on the half conscious horse as Shannon wagged her tail.

As my kids grew, Hallie became more helpful and Willie became more of a handful. Fortunately, I had babysitters who could keep pace with Willie: Heidi the goat, Cricket the coyote and Shannon the Irish setter.

We couldn't find Cricket one day. She was spayed and had never shown any interest in running off with coyotes from the national forest behind the clinic. The farmers in the area prided themselves in either shooting coyotes or, in winter, running them over with their snowmobiles. Because wheat fields took up ninety-five percent of the area, coyotes were no problem as predators, except for the occasional chicken coop raid. A common sight outside Pullman was to see one or two coyotes following a farmer plowing his field. This was beneficial to the farmers, as the coyotes ate the rodents

Dr. Marinel Popple and Cricket

Outstanding Young Women Of America
—with pet coyote, Cricket

Nominationed as one of the Outstanding Young Women of America, Pullman Herald, November 4, 1971

that ate the wheat, but that natural balance of nature never entered the minds of most of those farmers. Two weeks went by and Cricket hadn't returned. For her protection, I'd sprayed her with a fluorescent pink paint and put a bright red collar, with rabies tag and my name and number on it. But that didn't help. On the fifteenth day, Cricket showed up on the front porch. She'd been shot and was near death. Her front leg was broken in seven places and gangrene had set in. She licked my hand and whimpered. She was so weak she couldn't stand. I gently carried her into surgery, starting her on an IV drip of fluids to combat dehydration and antibiotics for the infection. I gave her glucose to increase her strength for surgery, which could not be postponed, then amputated her leg above the elbow, hoping she was strong enough to recover.

Nature has its reasons for making the coyote a survivor despite man's onslaught. Cricket was no exception. She regained her strength and soon became quite agile on three legs. We counted our blessings, as she'd become an important part of our family. I contacted the farmer who shot her and worked out a deal—he'd call me if Cricket returned to his farm and I'd buy him a bucket of Kentucky Fried Chicken every week.

Shannon was now seven and was not to be outdone by Cricket. The Irish setter began limping on the same front leg Cricket had lost. X-rays showed Shannon had a malignant bone tumor that, if allowed, could kill her if it metastasized to the lungs. The next day, I amputated Shannon's right foreleg. The big setter was not as agile on three legs as her friend Cricket but she rarely left the coyote's side. Clients often did a double take when greeted by these two furry tri-pods! If they were gone too long, my friend who owned the local radio would announce: "If anyone sees a three-legged coyote and a three-legged Irish setter, please call the local animal hospital."

When Hallie and Willie started school, Cricket and Shannon did not adjust well to their absence. I got a call from the school about them being on the playground with the children. School was almost over so the teacher agreed to let the canines remain until class was dismissed. When the bell rang two happy children were escorted home by their best playmates! The teacher was a friend and decided to let Cricket and Shannon come to the playground at three o'clock, just in time to walk their children home.

Veterinary hospitals in big cities have several ways to dispose of dead pets if owners don't want to bury them at home. The clinic's property was large enough to accommodate a place for dead pets, but individual graves were out of the question because of the hard, and often deeply frozen, ground, so we dug a trench six-feet deep and ten-feet wide behind the clinic that would accommodate animal bodies and kennel cleanings. Layer upon layer of earth would cover the burial pit, and when that trench was filled, a new one would be dug next to it. The pit always bothered me but it was a necessity.

I awoke to four inches of new snow one cold morning. It lightly dusted the iced-over pit, which was filled to the brim with months of rainwater and thawing snow and ice. The fresh snow covered the sheet of ice like vanilla icing on a cake. Our nearest neighbor lived a quarter mile to the east. They'd groomed their 4-H steer with great pains, preparing it for the winter fair. His red, curly coat, shampooed and rinsed, was carefully combed to give him a blockier look. His tail was combed at the end, in the shape of a ball. The five children who helped raise the steer were proud and hoped for a blue-ribbon win. The father prodded the large animal to walk up the truck's loading chute so they could haul him to the fair for the morning weigh-in. The steer bolted and rushed backwards when he saw the truck. He broke through the corral and headed for freedom, which unfortunately, was in the same direction as my clinic. With his grooms in pursuit, the steer became more excited and the farther he ran, the closer he got to the clinic. Dogs in the hospital runs started barking and the steer bolted sideways. He hit the ice-covered pit and sank, out of sight, into the dark hole. Of all the places in the whole countryside he could have headed, this steer picked the six-by-ten gravesite. Its walls were too steep to climb. He couldn't get any solid footing. Only his horns, eyes and nose were visible. From one horn, dangled the remains of a dead yellow cat; an old spotted dog draped around the other. The poor beast was frightened, cold and becoming exhausted from his struggle to free himself. The children's father went home to get a tractor. Upon his return, he wrapped a chain around the steer's horns and tried to pull the half-ton animal out. The pit's steep walls ruined that plan. It became apparent that someone had to get into the icy grave and wrap a rope around the steer's body. The father slipped into the icy water, his loud, abrupt language indicating how unpleased he was with this situation. Remembering all the practical jokes this guy had played on me over the last five years, I was enjoying the scene. Only the steer had my sympathy. One of the sons drove the tractor forward until the rope and chain tightened; another handed his father a hot shot to jolt the steer into action. The steer sank back into the pit. Another chain was found to wrap around the steer's abdomen. Forward the tractor lurched, as the cattle prod gave the steer a new desire to escape as it wildly dug into the dirt walls. Slowly, the exhausted bovine emerged. The father grabbed its tail, sliding on his belly up and over the pit as a dead cat rolled off his back. The poor steer was dragged home by his horns, the once fluffy ball at the end of his tail dangling with mud and ice.

Hai Karatie at 1 year old

9

THE HORSE SHOW CIRCUIT

"**M**y practice continued to grow, and with help from a bank loan, I built a sixteen-stall metal barn with an indoor arena, a viewing room, office and piped-in music. My black bay Arabian stallion Hai Karatie was now well known in the Northwest for his many wins and was desired for his stud service. I needed a facility to house the visiting mares. The barn would also provide a place to train horses during the cold, wet winters. Hitan, now twenty-seven years old, was a trust worthy mount for friends and the kids. Willie enjoyed entertaining his friends with Hitan's many tricks.

We enjoyed the Arabian horse show circuit and our horses did well. We had a four-horse trailer with a sleeper in the front. The kids and I would cuddle up after a long day of grooming and showing horses in places like Montana, Idaho, Washington and Canada. Hallie had been riding since in-utero and as soon as she could sit up, rode behind me on Hitan. As she was nearly born on a horse, she was a natural equestrian. She won many championships with her sixteen-hand Arabian gelding, Karrage, that she showed as a hunter-jumper and a western pleasure horse. She looked like a little blonde peanut on that big horse of hers, but they made a good team. Her half-Arabian mare became the state's champion halter mare and went on to become reserve champion halter mare of Canada! Willie also showed his horse, an Arabian gelding, but not with the success of his sister. Despite show riding lessons,

it was not in Willie's DNA to pace his horse in a slow steady gait. Willie only knew fast and faster. He would race his gelding around the show arena at three times the pace of the other junior exhibitors. At the state championship show he raced so fast, his gelding fell and slid across the arena. Straightening his hat and pulling it down so far that his ears stuck straight out, he climbed back on and again took off at a run. The ring steward had to stop him, and hold his horse in the center of the arena, as the other exhibitors finished the class.

Reserve Champ — Hallie Poppie, and her horse, Handywyn, have been winning several horse shows throughout the Pacific Northwest. Hallie holds the Reserve Championship trophy won at the Canadian Nationals in Calgary, Alberta, two weeks ago. —Herald pho¹

Hallie, a natural equestrian

Willie only knew fast and faster.

Between classes, Willie played under the grand stands. The show announcer would say, "Dr. Poppie, Willie is under the grandstands eating gum again." His jowls would be full, and he would refuse to spit out his treasures. He apparently developed a healthy immune system, as he never suffered from childhood diseases. The show circuit gave the children a healthy lifestyle. They played with many children their age and the adults doted on them. Best of all, I got to spend quality time with them day and night.

I ordered a semi-truck of hay from an Idaho hay broker. He quoted me a price I could handle. When the truck arrived, I was told a much higher price. I needed the hay, but wasn't about to pay the higher price. My friends came to the rescue. They hid behind the barn and unloaded the hay while I stalled the truck driver in my office, slowly counting out coins we'd gotten from the bank just for this. The driver got irritated and wanted to leave but I'd locked the door to my office and just kept on counting out the money. I gave him what we'd originally agreed upon. He refused to unload the hay for that. "Fine," I said. "Where I come from, a deal is a deal, so give me back my money and be on your way." One of my cohorts opened the door and the man walked back to his empty semi-truck.

The hay bales were thrown every which way and my unloading gang yelled, "Justice has been served! Beer party tonight!" The driver grinned. "You're right," he said. "My boss has been cheating on every load this spring. I'll be back for the beer party!"

Hallie and Willie in the state championship halter class

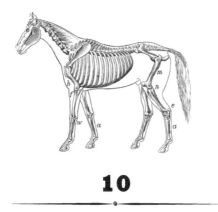

10

VETERINARY RESEARCH

A two-month old Arabian foal in Idaho was sick and wouldn't respond to my treatment. It died and I took it to the veterinary pathology department for an autopsy. The department was one of the forerunners to work with immune deficiency diseases. The foal had abnormal thymus and spleen tissue, which had been found in children with a similar fatal genetic immunodeficiency. The National Institute of Health, therefore granted a large sum of money to the veterinary research team in hopes of finding a cure for these children. I was asked to join the team as a research associate. It was an intense and exciting time. Vets with Ph.Ds conducted the lab work, while I did the field-work collecting blood samples throughout Canada and the United States from newborn foals. I also went to various horse clubs, educating them on the immune disease, treated affected foals and purchased dams and sires of affected foals. I acquired twenty mares and two stallions that had produced foals having this fatal immunodeficiency. The outcome of our work showed the disease was inherited as a recessive trait, that it occurred in both sexes and would skip generations. I published several articles in the veterinary medical journals describing this genetic disease. Our research lasted five years. It took the discovery of DNA linkage to find a genetic marker in carrier horses and eventually end this fatal disease through selective breeding.

11

NOTHING LEFT OF NOTHING
IS NOTHING

Professionally my life was good with my children, the research, the veterinary hospital and the breeding and training barn. Twice, I was nominated as one of the "Outstanding Women of America." Despite all the positive aspects of my life, I was suddenly in a downward spiral. My thirteen-year marriage was on the skids. There were too many people in the marriage and not enough love. The relationship became violent. The townspeople knew more about my marriage than I did! For nine years I'd been paying the mortgage on the clinic and the barn, but didn't know my husband had used them as collateral for his construction business, which unbeknownst to me was going broke. The bank repossessed all our assets, including our beautiful new house on the hill, my hospital and the barn. The money from our joint savings account disappeared when my husband and his friend went to the orient. This friend later called me and confirmed what I thought to be true. The judge awarded the kids and the house furniture to me. After the court order and prior to going to the orient, my husband hired his construction crew to remove every piece of furniture from our home and hide it in an apartment. After visiting my dad in Montana, the kids and I came home to an empty house. Asking a friend to help me, we broke through the back window of the apartment, loading all the furniture into my truck and horse trailer. A neighbor called 911 " burglary in process." Hearing the sirens, we raced from Washington to Idaho with a state trooper in hot pursuit. One chair of my dinning set flew out, hitting a passing car's windshield. As soon as we crossed the Idaho state line we hit the country roads and safely hid my trailer full of belongings in a friend's barn, to be retrieved later and hauled to Tucson.

Nothing left of nothing is nothing. My son and daughter were the only good results from a bad marriage. Leaving Washington was my only option. I gathered the kids, my Arabian stallion Hai Karatie, my ferret, our Australian sheep dog, and our calico cat that had kittens en route. We said goodbye to the graves of Shannon and Oliver, leaving Cricket the coyote, Heidi the goat, and my beloved stallion Arabian stallion Hitan, now twenty-seven, with friends. Some unknown vision told me to head south toward Mexico. We hauled our few possessions in our four-horse trailer. The full moon pulsated, as Mexican music played late into the night, guiding me in my southward journey. Although we'd lost most of our material possessions, I had three blessings no one could take from me: my children, my education and my guardian angel. Arriving in Tucson, we had very little money so slept in the horse trailer.

12

GODS GREATEST GIFTS ARE UNANSWERED PRAYERS

I was amazed at Arizona's desert's beauty. Its wide valleys, high rugged mountains, and incredible plants captivated me. The area had a Western flare I'd missed since leaving Montana. Maybe this life-altering situation was meant to be.

We found a cheap basement apartment to rent. What a contrast to the elegant, home we'd left behind. We couldn't afford furniture so the three of us slept on the floor, on my surgery drapes. One night I found a butcher knife under the surgery drapes. Asking Willie about it, he replied, "It's to save you from the raperers mom! Some boys convinced Willie to write the F word on the outside of the apartment buildings. A knock at the door revealed the manager holding Willie by one ear and the spray paint in his other hand. "What does the F word mean?" asked Willie. "It means we don't have anywhere to live," I replied. Back to the horse trailer we went until I found part-time work in a small-animal clinic and soon got hired on fulltime. We celebrated my income by going out to eat at our first Mexican restaurant. "Why are those people eating their napkins?" Hallie asked. I couldn't give her an answer then, but it didn't take too long before tortillas, became a common part of our lives.

The Tanque Verde valley

13

A PLACE IN THE SUN

The Arizona sky was an all-or-nothing sky, much like Montana, but there was no twilight. The sun seemed to tumble out of the sky as darkness quickly overtook the sunset. The majestic mountains gave me renewed strength. A forty-five minute drive could take you ten thousand feet up the mountain. Traveling this winding road, the view was breathtaking. From the wide valley floor, the ascent began. Thousand of cacti, all shapes and colors, including thousands of giant saguaro, covered the desert and rolling hills. A little higher up, junipers and cedars flourished among wild, craggy rock formations. Further up, the ponderosa pine forest and lush grass grew. I learned this forest was part of the Mogollon Rim, where the world's largest stand of ponderosa pine grew. And best of all, in this forest, was a ski hill. It wasn't an Olympic hill like we were used to, but it had snow and was an unexpected treasure. Hallie and I soon had weekend jobs, teaching skiing. Several small lakes dotted the valley floor below. Enjoying snow skiing one day and, within a short drive, water sports the next was a bonus. The valley didn't have distinct seasons like the north, but a trip up the mountains provided access to all the seasons in one day.

I joined a hiking club and conquered many Arizona peaks. Twice I was trapped at high elevations by sudden storms. In the rugged Chiricahua Mountains, where Apaches once roamed, darkness and snow fell before I could descend the trail. A Forest Service cabin provided shelter after forced entrance through a window. The next morning bought sunshine and warmth for my hike down. Another climb, this time to a summit of twelve thousand feet, was interrupted by an unexpected spring snow storm. The water in my canteen froze. Wrapping myself in a sheet of plastic, I waited out the long, cold night. To my surprise, the next morning was warm and sunny and thousands of ladybugs covered the rocks. My hiking trips provided interesting friends and I no longer felt lonely. Willie made a metal carving with a map of the mountains I'd climbed. It's one of my treasured possessions.

Money slowly began to build up in my savings from work at the small animal hospital. We dreamed of having our own home in an area next to the washes and mountains. Driving around, after work, I came across a new but deserted home. Spanish in design, it sat on five acres near a big wash and a fifty-thousand-acre national monument. A "For Sale" sign hung on the gate. The realtor said the owners had divorced and were desperate to sell. I needed five thousand dollars for a down payment and, with the help of a friend's loan, we had a home. It was white with a red tile roof, had four-thousand square feet of space, four bedrooms, a modern kitchen, sunken living room and a big family room with a fire place. All the furniture, dishes and linen had been left behind, which was a godsend as I had spent all our savings on the down payment. It didn't take long to figure out why the previous owners had left in such a rush. Pulling weeds in front of the house one day, I found what I thought was a large plot of stinging nettles. I began pulling them without much thought. Two acquaintances dropped by and asked me about the plants. I warned them not to touch the stinging nettles, which would leave white, itchy blotches on the skin. Laughing they said, "That's marijuana. You've got the "Mother Lode" in your front yard!" The next day, Willie called me while I was at work. "Mom, I found bags of white powder and funny-looking pipes in the kitchen drawer." We'd never experienced illegal drugs, but the kids recently had learned about them in school. I wanted them to decide how to dispose of them. "Let's bury them in the desert," Hallie said, so off we went with our shovel and collection of drugs. "I think I could sell them at school for a lot of money," Willie exclaimed, as we were digging a hole. We started talking about the harm they could cause and the kids decided we should call the sheriff and give him the drugs instead. To me, this was a good decision. The amount of drugs even surprised the sheriff as he explained his deputies had raided the house several times, one time finding guns with the drugs.

Their illegal lifestyle had afforded me a new start to life, and slowly the five acres were transformed into an equine facility for training horses and boarding visiting mares. I also acquired a group of colorful, fun, loyal and helpful friends. They consisted of Shorty the Mississippi Gambler, Nacho the crippled Apache Indian, George the handsome Greek, and Stubby, the double leg amputee. True friends, through thick and thin, they required no payment other than beer! The empty cans fortified the cinder blocks in the sixteen stalls we built. Painted white to match the house, the stalls were arranged in a courtyard formation around a show arena. There was no lack of sand for mortar and I soon became a master at applying a plaster finish.

Shorty (left) and George the Greek

Pen and ink drawing, Carolie

14

ROCK FOOTED LITTLE HIPPY

Hello, is any one home?" the voice woke me from my first night's sleep in our new home. There she sat, a skinny, pretty, barefoot blond with a floppy straw hat, sat bareback on her little sorrel mare. "Hello, my name is Carolie. I live on the other side of the wash." She explained. She would be my first new friend in Tucson. We had a lot in common, and from that day on, we shared a lot of adventures. Her four children were near in age to Hallie and Willie. Carolie knew the desert well, as she had been born and raised in Tucson. For being so small, she sure had big feet. Running through the desert barefoot was natural for her. We enjoyed hiking, riding, and art together.

Carolie suggested we hike Havasupi Canyon, on the south rim of the Grand Canyon with our kids. We planned to camp when we reached the water twelve miles below the rim of the Grand Canyon. The hike was steep, like walking off a crater on the moon. Finally arriving, we walked through an Indian village. A large group of Havasupi Indians had gathered for their annual rodeo. Crow Indians from Montana had been flown in by helicopter to participate in the rodeo, as no roads existed. Traveling through the Indian village we reached the beautiful aqua blue pools of water fed by a tributary to the Colorado River. A rope hung from an old cottonwood tree, providing a great swing into the cool beautiful turquoise pools. As the sun was setting, we rolled out our sleeping bags in preparation for a star filled night. A Forest Service ranger appeared, asking to see our permit. " A permit, why a permit?" No one had informed us the necessity for a permit. The ranger rudely told us to leave. It was dark and we had a steep twelve-mile climb out of the canyon.

Like in a John Wayne movie, the moon was rising over towering rock walls, as Indian drums sounded up and down the valley. Indians were everywhere. Having young blond Willie and three beautiful high school age girls with us, we stood out in the moonlight like fire flies. Tammy, wearing a tight white tee shirt that said Aloha, was the center of attraction. Some big buck, that had consumed too much firewater, jumped out of the brush and grabbed her. After rescuing her, we dressed her in a black hooded sweatshirt and hid behind the trees. The drums beat louder and faster. The Indians were in a drunken state of celebration. Several more Indians became aware of our presence and threatened our departure. Traveling through a deep

Mooney Falls, Havasupi, Grand Canyon

thicket of trees, we escaped the moonlight and began a dark assent up the steep twelve-mile rocky trail. Tammy hit her foot on a large bolder, resulting in the splitting of her toe. Gamely she hiked on, as the tom toms beat on to the pulsating moon. Putting some distance between Indian village and us, the full moon now guided our way. Exhausted, we reached a cave near the trail, where we welcomed the soft dirt and fell into a deep sleep. Suddenly, awakened by some one stumbling over us, was an old Indian woman, seeking shelter in the cave. Now, wide-awake, we continued our long climb toward our truck and to safety leaving the beating of the Indian drums in the canyon below.

Having our own home and stable area, Hallie and Willie joined 4-H. My brother Bud had given Hallie a beautiful heifer and Willie chose to raise and show a pig. The time to take them to the county fair had arrived. We borrowed a small trailer and loaded the Heifer and Bacon the pig. The trailer seemed to jerk and pull with difficulty. After a couple blocks of hauling we stopped to check the trailer. The back door had swung open. Hallies' heifers' hind legs and bloody hoofs were on the asphalt as Bacon stood between the heifers' front legs wondering if he should jump or ride it out! Murphy's Law made sure two other families going to the fair had witnessed this event. All the miles I had hauled four horses with no problem, and now this, the new veterinarian wanting to start a large animal practice had created a disaster. By the time we reached the fair grounds, we were the talk of the day. Hallie was scheduled to show her heifer in three days. Miraculously, it recovered from its lameness and she won first place in showmanship! Willie loved Bacon and slept with him every night. Dressed in his white shirt, green pants and tie he entered the ring with his show cane in hand. Like the horse show ring he wanted to go fast and faster. The cane was replaced as Willie booted Bacon to speed up his pace. Willie was awarded last place for showmanship, but his pig won the blue ribbon for type and conformation.

15

YOO HOO THE OWL

Imagine an oversized cotton ball with big, blinking yellow eyes. That was what the one-day-old great horned owlet that had fallen from its nest looked like as my vet tech handed it over to me. I'd raised Oliver the owl from an infant. I would save this baby! After about a week, Yoo Hoo took her first tiny, teetering steps. The next week, she ran across the carpet, flapping her wings. After a month, she was airborne and flying around our house. She was growing fast and soon her wingspan stretched beyond six feet. Like Oliver, she had to tip sideways to fly down the four-foot wide hallway. Yoo Hoo came and went as she pleased, spending a lot of time in the courtyard. She didn't want to leave. On warm evenings when the neighbors were barbecuing, she'd return from her adventures with steaks and ribs. The neighbors loved to tell me about the beautiful owl that graced their outdoor parties; I never said a word but enjoyed many fine meals. I often had court-yard parties around our swimming pool. Yoo Hoo's silent flights, from her rooftop perch to my guests' dinner plates, often left the guests bewildered and deciding they'd had too much to drink.

George the Greek and me

Yoo Hoo went with me on most of my calls. She sat on top of the seat, facing backward, turning her head one hundred eighty degrees to look at the road ahead. Nothing seemed to ruffle her feathers. After a long day of visiting patients, I stopped at my cowboy bar where George the Greek and Nacho were having beers, along with Daisy the cocker spaniel who sat on her stool at the end of the bar. I knew most of the patrons and had become good friends with the owner. She loved Yoo Hoo and let the owl walk up and down the horseshoe-shaped bar. She fluffed her feathers and blinked at her friends. Daisy the dog paid little attention; the customers were delighted, except for one. Yoo Hoo had backed into his bourbon and water and had turned it into a White Russian! The irate man grabbed Yoo Hoo and swung her in the air. George the Greek leaped from his bar stool, punching the man so hard, that he slid down the opposite wall. "Don't you ever touch her owl again," he yelled, "or it'll be the last thing you do." Cheers broke out up and down the bar and Yoo Hoo helped us dance the night away.

The summer of Yoo Hoo's second year was scorching hot. While sitting outside on the picnic table, she collapsed to the ground. I rushed her into the house, spread her giant wings out on the pool table, administered IV fluids into her wing, and prayed. She was tough and pulled through but her daytime activities were restricted to the house. The summer of her third year was too hot for her as well. Some giant cottonwood trees along the nearby wash provided cool shade and I'd seen several great horned owls there. With my heart close to breaking, I drove Yoo Hoo several miles up the wash and turned her loose. She wouldn't leave the truck, so I carried her into the cottonwood grove, sat her on a branch and sadly drove away.

Miley and Yoo Hoo

Calvin Swine

16

CALVIN HITS THE SLOPES

Calvin Swine, my three-week-old pot bellied pig, was too little to stay home alone. We were still bonding and he would sleep with me for another week. Wyetta, my brother Buds' daughter came from Montana to visit. She was special, cute as a bug, with Buds' great laugh. He had named her Wyetta after his hero, Wyatt Earp. Skiing in Tucson had closed, but the ski hill on the Apache reservation would be open. Wyetta and I packed up little Calvin, and headed for the reservation. We would ski for two days and sleep in the back of the pick up truck. Calvin was secure in his little plastic carrier. Spring skiing was perfect: bright warm sun and plenty of snow. Calvin slept with us in our sleeping bags that night. The next morning promised another great day on the slopes. Packing our lunch, we decided to take Calvin up the hill with us. The three of us would picnic on the mountain. Calvin would be safe in his carrier and easy to carry up the chair tow. After several runs, we found a perfect spot for lunch. Letting Calvin out to eat with us and play in the snow we relaxed in the bright sun. Never having seen snow before, Calvin became pretty excited, as he dashed too and fro, rutting through the soft white powder. Suddenly he jumped into his plastic carrier. It shot down the mountain, gaining speed at a rapid pace. Flying over moguls, he screamed like only a pig can scream. Barely missing skiers he flew down the crowded hill screaming at the top of his lungs. Startled skiers fell and ran into each other. Wyetta and I were in hot pursuit. Finally he plowed into some deep snow next to a log cabin. Several little Indian kids ran out to see him. Calvin quickly recovered from his ordeal and was happy to play in the snow with the Indian children.

Sonoran Desert cactus

17

SECRETS OF THE SONORAN DESERT

My stables were completed by spring. Karatie could now come home from the boarding stable. Horse owners were booking their mares to him for that breeding season. He and I learned the desert together. Our first ride off the property was through the desert. There were no trails to follow, but Karatie quickly learned how to avoid barrel cacti by carefully side stepping them. Cholla cacti, also called "jumping cactus" were a different story: Any slight brush against them sends spiny barbs into the passerby. Suddenly, Karatie tucked his tail and bucked his way through the desert. I couldn't believe what was happening; he'd never bucked with me. Trembling, he stopped and planted all fours. I slid off and examined him. His tail was clamped between his hind-quarters. Close examination revealed a ten-inch cholla embedded between his hind legs. Every time I tried the pull it out, it "crawled" to a new spot. He knew I was trying to help but was in so much pain that I tied him to a palo verde tree and raced home to get a sedative and some forceps. I removed the cholla and learned to carry a comb to flip off cholla cacti when I rode.

The desert brought constant changes. Saguaro cacti stood like sentries with their many arms. At the end of those arms grew delicate white flowers that ripened into a sweet red fruit harvested by the Indians. I loved riding with Nacho the Apache. He knew the desert well and we rode to hidden water holes through secret passageways. He taught me how to safely peel and eat the Prickly Pear cacti and how to make jelly from its fruit. On one ride along a steep trail, Nacho reached down from his horse, gathered a handful of red fruit off a Saguaro, and popped it into his mouth. I did the same. It was so sweet in my parched mouth, but then my mouth began to burn. Ants crawled out and stuck to my face. I spit out ants and fruit alike. Nacho continued to eat the red fruit as the ants crawled out of his mouth and covered his face. He didn't seem to care, flashing me a big, toothy smile.

The desert was abundant with life. Reptiles, especially lizards, were ever present. Some were small and fat, some thin and striped and quick as a wink. My favorites were the big blue-green lizards that did "push-ups" as they sunned themselves on the hot desert floor. Snakes were abundant as well. There were many non-venomous snakes like the checkered garter snake, the western hognose, the king snake and, my favorite, the coachwhip snake, an extremely fast snake that comes in two colors—black or florescent pink. When I saw the first of these pink snakes crossing the road, I thought I was hallucinating. Rattlesnakes are common too. The western diamondback is a heavy-bodied snake that can be aggressive, their venom deadly to man or beast. The Mojave rattler is even more aggressive with venom that kills almost instantly. One of the most interesting rattlers is the nocturnal sidewinder. It's smaller, appears to have horns, and leaves a distinct side-winding track in the sand.

Shortly after removing the cholla from Karatie, I learned firsthand how painful they are. They seem to crawl across their victim. Willie and I decided to clear out some cacti to make room for a riding arena. Many large cholla and other types of cacti grew in the front part of the property. We'd hook a long chain around the cholla, then to the truck's bumper as Willie drove the truck forward, pulling them out of the ground.

After thirteen years in gloomy Washington, I became a sun worshipper. Never wearing a hat, sun screen or sun glasses in Arizona, I absorbed every sunbeam's UV rays possible. I wore my skimpiest bikini to get the near-total sun experience. We had only one large cholla left to drag out. Willie jumped the truck forward and the cactus flew through the air. I knew from the experience with Karatie to stand back from those cacti, but a spiny, foot-long section impaled me across my very bare midriff. The pain was excruciating! My muscles twitched in reflex to the pain as the cholla "crawled" up and down my abdomen. Willie retrieved a hammer, screwdriver and pliers from the garage, wanting to help, but each time he tried to pull it off me, it sunk its thorns deeper into my skin. "Bring me some whiskey, Willie," I said. "I can't stand the pain." I practically drained the bottle, sinking to the ground, the cactus still firmly lodged in me. Willie ran to the street and waved down a motorist. "My Mom needs help," he told the driver. "She's on the ground with a cactus in her belly!" The man looked at me in disbelief, but he and Willie dislodged the cholla by each grabbing an end with pliers and pulling straight up. It didn't come out easy—my skin stretched as far as it could go with the cactus until it finally tore out. Whiskey had helped numb the pain, as I remained on the hot desert sand, thinking of soft, green grass and pine trees in Montana.

Tammy and Hallie with Dad, watercolor by author

18

MY FAMILY BLESSINGS

Life with the kids in Tucson was fun: skiing, riding, and trips to Mexico. Willie's sixth grade science teacher took the class rappelling in the Catalina Mountains. They made history by being the first to complete the Tyrolean traverse across a long canyon. Their science project was to collect scat from mountain sheep to determine their diet. Willie became a good soccer player, playing for the local team and winning the state championship. A family of five boys befriended him. They were definitely all boy, and Willie mixed well with them. Daring and too full of adventure, two of these young boys died from terrible accidents. The first of Willie's friends died from a cave-in of the hideout they were digging in the sandy bank of the wash. The second, was lost to a pipe bomb they were building to celebrate the end of the school year. Willie was a survivor. He too, had an over-worked guardian angel. Willie's desire to drive, never ceased. At age thirteen, without permission, he borrowed Hallie's first car, a new silver Mustang, and drove it through a barbwire fence. Willie took classical guitar lessons

Willie age 14

with mixed results. When he was fourteen, he returned to Washington to learn the construction business. His empty room consisted of KISS posters, strobe lights, and the sign on the door that said "Danger Zone, Mother Do Not Enter!"

Hallie continued her dancing lessons, earning her toe shoes in ballet. She tried out for John Denver's traveling musical, "Up With People," and traveled to South America and the Navajo Indian reservation, where she stayed in a Navajo hogan. Dancing and singing her way around the world, her final performance was to provide the half-time entertainment at the Super Bowl in

Detroit. I sat at home, watching her on television as she danced back and forth across the screen in a teeny-weenie, yellow polka-dot bikini. Hallie was a good student and well-liked by her classmates; she would not dish the dirt with the rest of the girls. She was elected cheerleader and student body president of her large high school. She went on

Hallie and her heifer

to the University of Arizona to receive her degree as a dietician. Joining her and living with us was her friend Tammy from Washington, who was sweet, smart and beautiful. Tammy shared adventures with me in Mexico and Havasupi canyon. My home was blessed with my two beautiful girls. Hallie later married and settled in Washington. Tammy married and moved to Phoenix. They both have two children, each a boy and a girl.

Hallie

Tammy

19

VERSITLE HAI KARATIE

There were a lot of horses in the Tucson area: western horses, hunters, jumpers, gaited horses, draft horses, ponies, mule and burros. Riding clubs and horse shows were commonplace. The Sonoran Desert was wide open for riding as meandering washes created unlimited open space. Usually dry with clean sand and lined by cottonwood trees, you could ride miles without a fence ever crossing your path. Winding trails through spectacular landscape easily could be accessed from our back yard, including fifty thousand acres closed to all motorized vehicles. Hai Karatie and I won our first competitive trail ride in this area. It was such a rush. I could see the other competitors raising dust in the distance as they raced to catch us. We were uncatchable as we raced across the desert, like cowboys and Indians I thought. I hadn't felt this happy and free since my childhood in Montana. As this was a two-day race, the racers camped together near some corrals. A dance was held in the corral that evening. A girl friend started screaming, "it's him, it's him, its Paul McCartney." I had no idea who Paul McCartny, the man sitting on the fence, was. Later I learned he was my neighbor, living just up the wash from our home. The next year I competed in the Tevis Cup Endurance Race—one hundred miles in one day, from Nevada to California, over the rugged Sierra Nevada Mountains. Considered the world's toughest endurance race, I was thrilled after Hai Karatie and I completed it in good condition.

Willie wanted to go on an endurance race with me. He rode the only full brother to Hai Karatie, Bay Baron. Being a junior, he was only allowed to race thirty-five miles. My race was fifty miles and in a different direction. I held my breath as Willie and Bay Baron took off. At the finish line I heard stories about a young blond boy who raced his horse at a very fast speed, passing the other racers. I was then told that they would see him down in a creek catching frogs or throwing rocks. His horse tied to a tree. Again he would pass them at break neck speed, over the mountain and out of sight. Completing my ride, I saw Bay Baron tied to a tree and covered with dried sweat. No one knew where his rider was or why the horse was not groomed. Every one looked for Willie. After my fourth check of the living quarters in our trailer, Willie was found so sound asleep under all the sleeping bags that he could barely wake up. Awards were given around the campfire that evening. To my total surprise, Willie won second place for the fastest time. He insisted that he go with me on the next endurance ride where he also placed well, despite his total lack of pacing his horse for the long distance. Fast and faster had been his forte since he learned to crawl and it always would be.

Since 1925, Tucson has put on the world's largest non-motorized parade. Draft horses

Hai Karatie and I winning first place in Best Mounted Division in Tucson's La Fiesta de los Vaqueros parade.

pulling stagecoaches and other elaborate wagons appear out of nowhere. Saddle horses of various breeds and Brahma cattle are ridden or driven along the crowd-packed route through downtown Tucson. Karatie and I entered. I found a black and silver parade saddle, made a century earlier by the Cog Shell Saddlery in Miles City, Montana, and dressed in Spanish attire. My beautiful Karatie was shiny black bay and kept time with the music, sure the marching band and pom-pom girls behind us were just for him. We won first place in the Best Mounted Division.

Karatie showed his stuff with that same kind of dignity and pride in the Arabian horse shows in Arizona. They featured the best Arabian horses in the world and Karatie took home many championships in western pleasure, reining, English pleasure and hunter jumper classes. He won enough national points to be awarded the national "Legion of Honor." Versatile and a crowd-pleaser, Karatie took Hallie and many other junior riders to championships, as well. At age thirty, he was still winning Class-A competitions. He produced more than five hundred foals. He'd never been sick or lame in his lifetime, until the day he suffered a stroke and died in my arms, at age thirty-six.

Hai Karatie winning one of many
Western Pleasure Championships

Canine nurses

20

VETERINARY PRACTICE IN THE LAND OF THE SUN

My ambulatory horse clients wanted me to treat their small animals too, so a small animal clinic was built. It wasn't elaborate, but adequate. Diseases not seen in most of the United States are prevalent in the Sonoran Desert. Valley fever, a fungal infection that comes from the soil invades, the lungs and bones and other organs of mostly dogs and man, but some times other species. Its' treatment is long and costly, often leading to death. Tick fever causes dogs to become anemic and can be deadly. Hard to control in the desert, the brown tick is a prevalent pest. Cattle ear ticks are found in cattle horses, dogs and cats. Screwworms are also a problem in the Southwest; they've killed thousands of cattle, horses and other animals. When first arriving in Tucson, small wooden, screened boxes were scattered throughout the desert. I asked what they were? They contained sterilized male screwworms as part of a successful government eradication program. The flies mate, but couldn't produce offspring. By the time I moved to Arizona, the state was nearly screw-worm free. Being a federal regulatory veterinarian, I was to report any federal regulated diseases that came my way. Any maggots suspected of being screwworms were to be sent to the state's veterinary diagnostic lab. Before Mother's Day, I collected some maggot specimens and boxed them up to go to the lab. For Mothers' Day, I purchased a see-through black negligee to send to Mom. The two boxes got mixed up. Mom got the screwworms and the lab had a sexy, black nightie! Moms' feelings were terribly hurt.

I heard rumors from the state lab about the only female large animal veterinarian in Tucson.

Other medical abnormalities common to the Sonoran Desert included rattlesnake bites, javelina wounds, toad poisonings and cacti impalements. The small animal population seemed to suffer almost as many medical afflictions as the horse population. My profession became more than full time as sixteen-hour days, night time emergencies and long, weekends were common.

21

EQUINE SURGERY CENTER

Horses suffered from many disorders found in the Sonoran Desert. I saw more equine medical emergencies in one week in the Tucson than I would see in a month in Washington or Montana. Many horses were overfed and under worked. Stalled in small pens, they ate sand out of boredom, and could accumulate up to two- or three-hundred pounds of sand in their colons. Another colon problem, often proving to be fatal, was hard, round mineral buildups called enteroliths. These "stones" endemic in the southwest, could weigh up to ten pounds and horses that couldn't pass them died of colic. Mesquite beans also caused fatal colic. The beans, if not eaten when wet, provided a good protein source for horses. Unfortunately, pen-raised horses often would over indulge on the beans that blew into their pens on wet, rainy days. The long fibers in the wet beans were like nylon threads that would "ball up" and block the large colon much like the sand and stones. Despite aggressive treatment with oil, IV fluids, and painkillers, many of the horses died a painful death. Surgically removing these various intestinal blockages was the only way to save them, but we were taught in vet school that colic surgery was not an option. I refused to believe this and, after studying with an out-of-state veterinarian who performed colic surgeries on horses, I decided to provide colic surgery in my practice. Tucson horse owners would then have the option to put their horses to sleep or have them undergo surgery. To provide this specialized surgery, I needed help and turned to my neighbor, Wendy, who was with the University of Arizona's Race Track Industry Program, an excellent horse trainer, smart, hard-working and up for the challenge. Her favorite TV program was MASH and she could fit into any emergency situation as these surgeries could be long, difficult and often unorthodox. She would be perfect. I hit my equine anatomy books with a vengeance and purchased a large animal anesthetic machine, a heart monitor, a large, padded rotating table and three thousand dollars of surgical instruments for the new equine surgical facility we were building. A client requested I euthanize their two crippled horses. After humanely putting the horses to sleep, Wendy and I practiced every abdominal surgery possible. After several hours of "gut puddling," the tallow company came to pick them up for disposal. The driver, who spoke only Spanish, looked startled as Wendy and I literally emerged from the horses' bellies. I think he said he was in a hurry, so we ended our exploratory surgeries as he winched the horses into the truck and drove away. We soon realized we'd left the surgical instruments inside one of the horses. The tallow plant was thirty miles across town and closed by the time I got there. The next morning found me looking through dead horses before they were ground into fertilizer. They all began to look the same and the stench was overwhelming. The many matcho Mexicans working at the tallow made comments I was happy I could not understand. Memories of the kill floor at the meat inspection plant flooded my mind. My search came up empty-handed and new instruments were ordered.

Mickey, a thirty-year-old Arabian gelding, was our first patient for colic surgery. When his owner called, saying she was bringing him to the hospital for colic, I assumed he was to be euthanized. He was old and his owner had a limited budget. "Oh no, please try to save him," Susan the owner said. "He's so special." Mickey was special. He came through surgery with flying colors, his big heart never missing a beat as we untwisted his colon. After recovery in our special, padded room, he was lead into intensive care. I slept on a cot next to his stall and kept him medicated throughout the night. The radio played country western music as I dozed in and out of sleep. Unlike my very first patient, the dying mouse, my first colic surgery was a huge success. After three days of "post op," Mickey went home. "I think he likes country western music," Susan said, writing a check for the entire bill. That afternoon, I delivered a radio to Mickey and tuned it to his favorite station.

Our next surgery was to save a mare with sever colic that would not respond to conventional treatment. She was nine months pregnant. Surgery was always long and difficult due to the fact that the large gas filled cecum emerged from the opening incision of all abdominal surgeries to a height far above my head. It looked like a schmoo. A suction apparatus was used to remove the gas, thus enabling me to see the surgical field. This surgery was even more difficult due to the large foal crowding her abdomen. Opening her colon I found an eight-pound enterolith, "intestinal stone". It was flattened on three sides, so I knew there would be at least one more. There were two more. The mare recovered from the anesthesia, but I was fearful that the six hours of surgery could cause her to lose her foal. A month later she delivered a healthy little stud colt with no complications.

With in a three-year period we performed eighty abdominal surgeries with a seventy-five percent success rate. Horses diagnosed early as surgical candidates did well. Horses that were already in a toxic condition were difficult to save. Some friends became involved. Realizing the immensity of these colic surgeries, they volunteered to assist. Our angel of mercy, Phyllis responded to our needs day and night. Helping with surgery all night, she would be the first each morning to check the post-operative status of each horse.

Finding we were capable of successfully performing these difficult surgeries fulfilled every dream I'd ever had of reducing suffering through my education in veterinary medicine. All the time, money and sacrifices to obtain my medical knowledge was finally rewarded. I had seen too many suffering horses die from colic. Horse owners could now choose between surgery and humane euthanasia.

22

AMBULATORY CALLS

Ambulatory calls could be cold in the winter, and always hot in the summer. I learned to wet my underwear and place it in the freezer the night before starting my summer farm calls. After treating my patients, I would dose my self with the water hose, leave the windows down and travel to my next call as a human swamp cooler. The air conditioner was not an option, as the temperature variation between the truck and the desert was too extreme.

One ambulatory horse call literally started out with a bang. Receiving a call for a colicky horse, my office help suggested I shouldn't go because the horse owner had a reputation for packing a big gun and little patience with vets. Not only had this feisty woman intimidated her neighbors, but City Hall as well. Neighborhood kids called her the Witch of the Forest. I couldn't leave a colicky horse without medical attention, especially on a hot, humid day, so I went, with a good dose of trepidation. The thick mesquite forest revealed a long row of pink block stalls and an old, rambling pink house. As I approached, I was greeted by a threatening yell: "Who the hell's there?"

When she saw I was the new horse doctor, she introduced herself. Sheila had thick gray hair, bowed legs, wore men's clothing, and was packing a forty-five Derringer. "Follow me!" she demanded. An old sorrel mare, named May, stood there, her abdomen distended, her head hanging down, as her tangled mane nearly touched the ground. I asked the owner to hold the twitch to restrain May as I inserted the long rubber hose up Mays' nose and down into her stomach. I was pumping two gallons of mineral oil into her when all hell broke loose! "Hey you dumb sons of bitches! Get out of my wash!" Sheila bellowed and fired off a bullet, passing close to my head. The four-wheelers sped away. May reared and bolted. I grabbed the startled horse, and began retrieving the oil and my sand-covered tools: stomach tube, bucket, twitch and vials of scattered medicine. The mineral oil I'd been pumping into May was now equally dispersed upon the horse, the desert sand and me.

"If you ever fire a gun again while I'm treating your horses, you can find yourself another veterinarian," I said, knowing my threat wouldn't change this woman's ways, as I'd heard her last vet had nearly lost his ear in one of these shooting episodes. "I'm really sorry," Sheila said. "But I can't let them run the wash. I'd shot out their tires if that mesquite limb hadn't been in the way." Without skipping a beat, she added, "Do you think May got enough oil?" I'd given May shots for pain and intestinal cramping so all we could do was wait. May had spent her life with Sheila and was a gentle friend to the old woman. She was well fed and, despite her appearance, was loved. In her twenty-five years by the wash, May had become a "rock hound," spending her spare time between breakfast and dinner eating sand and small rocks. Sand colic was a way of life for her. She had it every month or so and always responded well to treatment. Passing a few gallons of sand and oil the day after treatment kept the old horse alive. "Sheila," I said, "May might not be a gold mine, but if I did some reconstructive surgery on her rectum and fed her mortar, we could start a brick factory and you could build more stalls!" She laughed. "I built all these stalls, and my house, by myself," she said. "I was married once but divorced the son of a gun on grounds of stupidity!" Sheila was my kind of woman—honest and direct. If I could survive long enough, I knew we'd become friends, the kind you never forget!

"You have to meet my other horses. Some need attention, too," Sheila said. We treated Gallon, a thirty-year-old quarter horse, for arthritis and a sole abscess. Chaco also got treated for a sole abscess. He was a liver chestnut quarter horse, approaching thirty. I saw ten other horses: seven quarter horses, two Arabian mares and one Arabian stallion, two-years-old and not halter broken. Two more of these horses had sores on their feet. The monsoon season had begun and the combination of rain-soaked soil in the manure-filled corrals and the constant humidity created the perfect conditions for growing bacteria. Thunderheads gathered, sounding their warnings. The one-hundred-ten-degree air was nearly unbearable. Horse flies looked for shade, buzzards circled the sky, and harvester ants increased their efforts to carry alfalfa and mesquite leaves to their underground tunnels, safe from the flooding that was sure to come.

"I wish it'd hurry up and rain," we both said in unison, as we sought the shade of a large mesquite tree. Lightning cracked, the sky broke open and the winds swirled. Willie, the dwarf Hereford bull with horns too big for his head, threw his nose toward the sky, rolled the whites of his bug-eyes and turned tail to the wind. The other cattle followed his lead. Horses raced back and forth in their stalls and five goats gleefully danced up and down on a fallen tree trunk. Sheila ran for the house to comfort her dogs, scared of the thunder and lightning. My parched body soaked up the rain like a barrel cactus; the

Sheila Ward

Sheila Ward, 89, passed away peacefully after a lifetime of inspiring, befriending, annoying and sometimes angering those she knew on March 15, 2004. One of the Tanque Verde Valley's early residents, she came to the area in the 1940's and found her true home. Sheila always did her own thing, in her own way (usually well armed). Her friends, family, animals and even those with whom she did not see eye-to-eye will truly miss one of life's great players. Sheila's legend will live on. A memorial service will be held at 9 a.m., Wednesday, May 12 at St. Augustine's Cathedral, 192 South Stone.

Sheila Ward's obituary

gnarled mesquite made a good backrest. Surrounded by giant cottonwoods and silvery sycamores that thrive along the washes, I felt no threat from the lightning, although I could see several nearby strikes. My long, hot summer burnout began to subside, as did the storm. The invigorating smells of the refreshed desert were strong. I'd already put in nine hours of work, but my energy was renewed, and the cool, quiet aftermath of the storm mesmerized me into a peaceful, thoughtful place.

The next week it was 117 degrees at noon! I was happy to be indoors, doing routine procedures in the small animal clinic. The phone rang. It was Sheila. "My cow's trying to calf. She needs a C-section," she told my office helper. "Tell her I can't come. I'm busy. I'm not a good cow doctor," I said. My helper shook her head. "She says if you don't come, she's coming to get you." I knew none of the other large animal vets in Tucson did cattle work and most of them were terrified of Sheila. Up to the clinic she drove her junk-filled, old truck—her machete and derringer on the dash. There was no escape!

I'd never done a C-section on a cow, but I had done more than fifty on horses during the time I was a research associate at the University. The geriatric Hereford cow was straining in heavy labor. "Can we get her under that shade tree?" I asked. "She won't budge," Sheila replied. "We have to do it here." Here meant under the glaring sun, in a pile of manure, on the hottest day I'd witnessed in Tucson. There was no cattle chute and she jumped away from me every time I tried to give her an epidural. My only choice was to try two drugs I gave to sheep and goats. Because of the size difference between a goat or sheep and a cow, I'd have to give several injections and closely monitor the cow to make sure she didn't wake up during surgery. The process was ridiculous, like a bad comedy. First, the anesthetics were administered and the cow dropped into a pile of manure. A lizard darted across her abdomen. Ants and flies were everywhere. I rolled her on her back, stabilizing her with rocks, then draped her with a large sterile sheet. After making a long, mid-line incision through her skin and into her abdomen, I cut into the distended uterus. The calf was large. It moved as I found it's hind legs, and began to pull it out. Mama began to move. "Give her the first drugs I gave you. Reach under the drapes and give them into her muscle," I instructed Sheila. "Hurry!" Sheila emptied the first syringe into the cow and soon she was still. I continued to pull the calf out. It was a huge, healthy bull calf, and Sheila was delighted. "He's beautiful," she said. "See, you're a good cow doctor." I had to sew everything back up and the old cow began to kick before I was finished. I told Sheila to shoot her with the second syringe of anesthetic. Sheila, caught up with excitement, gave the dose to the newborn instead. "No!" I screamed. "Give the calf CPR while I finish sewing up your kicking cow!" I never sutured so fast or sweated so hard into a surgery incision. Finally it was closed and I went to Sheila and the overdosed calf. I tried to swing it, performed CPR and gave it a shot of antidote, but the newborn died. Sheila was devastated. Mama cow wandered off, through the manure and into the mesquite trees, dragging my surgical drapes with her, as I had not had time to undo the towel clamps.

Sheila and I bonded for good after that. She wouldn't call any other vet unless I was out of town. Appearances are deceiving: old gruff and rough Sheila was a direct descendant of British royalty on her father's side and Spanish royalty on her mother's. She was well-bred, well-read and spoke several languages. She came from "old money" but hid it under her old clothes and beat-up vehicles. She was a true gem—rare and special. She never talked about her famous friends but there were many. Once I found her sitting in her courtyard, chatting with author Larry McMurtry, who won the Pulitzer Prize for his "Lonesome Dove" series. With no close family, Sheila would get lonely on holidays like Thanksgiving and Christmas. That's when I'd invite her to join the kids and I for dinner. She combed her hair and wore bright-red lipstick. As we sat down for our holiday meal, she pulled out her Derringer and placed it next to her fork. Startled at first, we got used to it. Willie thought it was cool! She had the table manners of a queen and entertained us with her intellect.

The combination of Sheila, Shorty, the Greek, Nacho and Stubbie, my double leg amputee friend, made my life more than interesting. Bringing a girl friend home from school, Hallie and her new friend approached as Stubbie and I worked to repair a fence. She introduced her friend to me and I introduced her friend to Stubbie. Hallie was so embarrassed that I had called him Stubbie. That was the only name I knew him to have. "Why can't you have normal friends, like other mothers have," Hallie asked, after her friend left. A few days later, she answered her own question saying, "I'm glad you don't have normal friends Mom, they're boring!" Shorty, Nacho and George the Greek and I often gathered together at the Cow Pony bar to dance. George was the best dancer but Nacho was sure he was. Nacho's crippled leg didn't slow him down. His only problem was he could not turn, so would dance me into a corner and just keep dancing. Spinning him on his good leg was the only means of escape.

23

PROUD FLESH, GREEK STYLE

A pack of dogs took down a client's foal, mutilating its hind legs. Sutures were placed where possible, but large areas of missing tissue required "tincture of time" to fill the gaping wounds. Horses rapidly produce scar tissue to heal leg wounds, as they depend on flight for their survival. Scar tissue often is too excessive and is surgically removed for cosmetic purposes. This was the case of the young foal. It developed a six-by-eight inch area of "proud flesh" two inches thick. Removing it, I took it home and placed it in my freezer to save for the equine science class, I taught at the college. In the meantime, George the Greek's mother came to visit, staying at my house. She was a tiny woman with bright red hair, and a heavy Greek accent. She loved cooking her Greek meals for us. Tonight I would teach my students about "proud flesh." Pre-surgical and post-surgical photos of the injured foal, would again be supported by the "proud flesh" exhibit. When I went to get it, it wasn't in the freezer. It had been there for five years. Where was it? I asked Stella if she had seen it? She was so proud of the special way she had prepared Mousaka and she had served it to us last night for dinner!

After moving from Greece to the United States, Stella lived a sheltered life in Cape Cod and was bewildered by the Wild West. George helped me breed our mares each evening. Stella, the proper and modest mama, would run out to the breeding shed yelling "you no a look George, you no a look!" Fergie my ferret loved to torment Stella. While she sat knitting, he would grab her ball of yarn and race madly down the hall with his prize. He lived in the bottom kitchen drawer, where he could see every one's feet. The cutting board pulled out of the counter above his drawer. Stella was making baklava, wearing slippers with no heal straps. We were all in the kitchen, when Fergies head peeked out from the bottom drawer and pulled her slipper into the drawer. "Where go a my slipper?" she yelled just as the second one disappeared! When the air ducts became inefficient, the cooling and heating company was called. Finding a hand full of yarn, the service man began to pull on it. Out came yards of yarn entangled in multiple stuffed animals and yes, Stellas' slippers.

Sheila's horses, cows, dogs and cats kept me hopping. Sometimes she'd call, saying it was an emergency when it wasn't. She just wanted company. One hot summer afternoon she asked me over for a beer by her pool. That sounded good. It had been a long day, with lots of patients. The pool was filthy, with floating garbage and black leeches. Like her horses, the beer was thirty-years old. It tasted like pure aluminum. "What are those things in the pool?" I asked, offering to take some back to the lab to determine the species. "Guess I'd better clean the pool," she replied. She never did.

It was time to vaccinate all her horses. Most were easy to handle, but the two-year-old stallion was another story. I told her we needed to halter him, hold him, and she needed to stand on the same side I was on. "Oh no," she said. "Anwar will stand still if I tell him to," Sheila said. "I'll just stand here and pet him while you give him his shots from the other side." Anwar didn't notice the first shot. The second one sent him flying across his stall and out the door. Sheila hit the block wall and slid down into the deep manure. Anwar raced back to his stall and ran over her a second time, then a third, as he headed out for his pen. Blood flew across the stall and covered the wall.

Her head was buried in manure. Pulling her up gently, I saw soft, gray matter flowing from the wound. Sheila raised her head. Her eyeglasses were on her chest. "Lord, help me. I haven't seen this well in years!" she exclaimed. "Are my brains falling out?" I raced to my truck, grabbed a bucket of Betadine and rolls of four-inch gauze. I washed the wound as well as possible, wrapped her head and literally dragged her into my truck. Calling 911 was not an option. I had no cell phone and she'd told me her dogs would kill any one who tried to enter her house. Propping her up in the seat, I sped to the hospital. She looked like a monster from a movie, her blood-and dirt-covered face wrapped in a brown turban.

The hospital was ten miles away. A road construction crew stopped us then waved us on after taking a look at Sheila. At the emergency entrance, Sheila yelled at the doctors, "Stay away from me! I want my vet to put my brains back in!" Intimidated at first, the emergency people got her sedated and hauled her off to surgery. Her tough, old hide recovered and she told everyone she could corner that I'd saved her life. One time I actually did. It was at a chicken dinner during a horse club meeting. I was seated one table away from Sheila and saw she was in distress, turning blue and gagging. She was choking. Knocking over a couple of chairs to get to her, I wrapped my arms around her and performed the Heimlich maneuver. A large piece of chicken propelled its way across the room as Sheila sank into her chair. After that, she liked telling how I saved her life twice.

Sometimes I wanted to strangle her. Sheila had eighteen dogs, mostly vicious and spoiled. One hot afternoon, she called, demanding I stop by and give her mean Rhodesian ridgeback a rabies vaccination. "That's not an emergency," I said. "I don't care," she screamed into the phone. "I want you to come now!" I ignored her until her incessant phone calls drove me to give in. I got to her house and she was waiting for me with Whiskey, the ridgeback that had twice before bitten me. I was hot, tired, and worn out by the long day. I didn't need any more aggravations and told her to wrap a leash around Whiskey's muzzle and hold the dog's head. "Whiskey won't bite you," she said. "Sure, and Anwar wouldn't run over you," I shot back, remembering that vaccination episode. She refused to muzzle the dog and, sure enough,

Whiskey sank her teeth into my arm when I tried to give her the rabies shot. Mad is too feeble a word for how I felt. I grabbed Whiskey's collar, flipped her around and kicked her through the mesquite forest, getting bitten two more times before the dog backed off. I hurled the vaccine at Sheila. "Give your own damn dog its damn shot and don't call me again!" Perhaps the most unprofessional moment of my career, it sure felt good, dog bites and all. I drove off, chastising myself: "Good work, Doc. You just lost your best client and her eighteen horses, dogs and cats. And you're going to miss her!" I got home after two more ambulatory calls. Sitting on the front porch was a bottle of Royal Crown whiskey and a note that read, "Whiskey is sorry." Attached was a drawing of a dog with tears running down her face!

Sheila was determined to make amends, she was going to take me to a Clint Eastwood movie and she wouldn't take no for an answer. We loaded into her junk-filled truck, stopping by the Circle K for fuel, her machete on the dash for all to see. Going into pay, she pulled her Derringer out of her pocket, along with her money, and set it on the counter. The young girl at the counter froze. Before she could hit the alarm button, I explained that it was not a holdup, that my friend had a permit to carry and was harmless. "Harmless," I thought. "Was I crazy?" Next stop was a pet store to buy dog food. She wanted to see the parrots. A teen-age boy walked up with a huge snake wrapped around him. He held the snake's head, swinging it back and forth at the frightened birds. The parrots screeched at the top of their lungs. Sheila whipped out her gun and held it to the boy's head. "If you make one more move with that damn snake, I'll blow its head off and yours too!" The startled teen screamed all the way through the store and out the door. "Damn kid, I should have shot the bastard!" Sheila muttered. "I am a dead aim with snakes. I shot several rattlers this week." I knew this to be true. I love Clint Eastwood movies, but this one seemed boring after our trip to the theater.

I had been happily single for ten years but, in a weak moment, decided to marry. The wedding was to be on horseback—me on my beloved Hai Karatie and the groom on his quarter horse. More than 200 people attended after being hauled across the desert by horse-drawn wagons to the wedding sight. I was to ride down the mountain from the north. The groom was to ride up from the south to meet me in the middle. The mesquite trees and cacti were decorated with wedding bells and flowers. Dad was there to give me away. Sheila was to fire her gun in the air to signal the start of the wedding. She had warned me not to marry. "It's a mistake, it's a mistake, it's terrible mistake," she had repeated over and over. Despite her objections, she stood in the front row waving her Derringer in preparation to shoot. Loudly she yelled, "If that bastard rides the wrong way, I'll shoot him out of his saddle!" The wedding guests stared at her in wonder, this might really get western! The bullet from her pistol cracked the sky and the wedding ceremony began. My three Australian shepherd cow dogs were decked out as flower girls, as were Hallie, Jackie, Leslie and Jeannie. A rattlesnake slithered down the bridle path, my false finger-nails fell off during the ceremony, and the preacher got drunk at the post-wedding party and landed in jail with a DWI by night fall. Sheila was right. It was a mistake!

Cow Boss

24

BACK TO MONTANA, WHERE MEN ARE MEN AND SHEEP ARE NERVOUS

For ten years I tried to prove Sheila wrong, but the marriage was like a hot bath—once you get in, it ain't so hot! I couldn't take another day. I called my wonderful friend Red, who was born and raised in the crazy mountains of Montana, not far from my Montana home. Red was half Indian and half Irish. He had red hair, freckles on his mischievous, handsome face and a cowboy build that was definitely a ten. He was orphaned and raised by the madams at the whorehouse thirty miles from my childhood Montana home. He could ride anything with hair on it. He would ride his wives' hunters and jumpers through the bar and jump them over cars. He was reckless, wild, fun and seemed indestructible. A semi-truck hit his pickup in front of a tavern south of Tucson. He was pinned in the crumbled mess for hours, as the "Jaws of Life" tried to free him. I was told he was dead and wept for my Montana friend all the way home. The next day he walked into my veterinary clinic with a big smile on his face. His guardian angel definitely worked overtime!

Red Rider, watercolor by author

When Red answered my call, I told him I had to get out of Tucson. Montana was calling me home. "You sound more than a little broncy. Bareback Jack and I will pick you up in the morning. We are heading north on the rodeo circuit. I hired a relief veterinarian, packed and took off early the next morning with Red Rider and Bareback Jack. Our first stop was the Phoenix rodeo, the second Cody, Wyoming, the third Jackson Hole, Wyoming. We played every Ian Tyson song ever written, drank beer, and laughed as the miles rolled by and Tucson was left in the dust. I felt like a freed bird that had been caged for ten years! Red rode saddle broncs and Jack rode bareback. They took turns winning and knew most of the cowboys along the trail. We tore up the floor at the rodeo dances and slept under the stars in the back of the pickup at night. Hints of the northern lights were pulling me home. West Yellowstone was soon in our taillights. I was dropped off at Jackie's condominium at Big Sky. She was so surprised to see me! It was June and it was snowing. We went sledding on the ski hill the next day. I rolled and played in the snow making snow-angels, sure I'd died and gone to heaven! I told Jackie about my failed marriage. She replied, I could have told you that when I was your maid of honor.

"We have to go to Stacy's bar tonight. It's Saturday and they will be having a dance."

Off we went. " I'm going to find me a cowboy," I exclaimed. "You just left one in Tucson and you're not even divorced yet" she replied. The horseshoe-shaped bar and worn out hardwood floor welcomed me with open arms. Just to think, my dad had boot-legged whiskey here during prohibition. I used my brother's fishing license to buy drinks before I was tall enough to see over the bar. Special high school friends sat in one corner. We were so glad to see each other. I bought the first round of drinks and stories of the good old days came easy. The sun was setting when a cowboy slid in through the swinging doors. He had dirty Levi's, a sweaty Marlboro shirt that stuck to his well muscled back, and a good, but dirty, silver belly hat. He was silhouetted in the doorway, standing hip shot, before sliding across the dance floor to the bar. Everyone seemed to know him. He had driven his tractor to the bar. Obviously having downed many beers while cutting his hay. He looked good standing hip shot at the bar. "Definitely a ten," I said to Jackie. "Hope he asks me to dance." She just shook her head. I had just had a major back surgery, including a fusion and titanium lumbar plating. I threw the doctor's advice to limit my physical activities to the wind when I left Tucson. I was going to dance with that cowboy if it killed me. Finally he headed in my direction. "Jackie, I'm going to marry that cowboy!"

"Oh boy," she replied. Arriving at our table he leaned over me and asked my girl friend to dance. "No thank you," she replied. He rocked back on his heels like Dwight Yokum, spun around, turned to me and asked me to dance. He was a great dancer despite his blood alcohol content! We danced several fast and slow dances. At the end of the last dance, he picked me up, putting amazing pressure on my lower back. Pain shot through me. I barely made it back to our table. I was taken to the hospital and laid in traction for three days wondering who was that sexy outlaw?

25

WHITE ROSES

The outlaw, after sobering up, was wondering who I was as well. My friends from the dance told him I was Buddy's little sister. "I used to know her," he told them. "I bought my first horse from their ranch!" A dozen white roses arrived with a note wishing me a speedy recovery, signed "love Gary." It was a done deal! Within a week I had moved into his two-room cabin up Bear Creek. We had no electricity and no plumbing. A green meadow full of wildflowers surrounded the old cabin. Deer with their new fawns played in the meadow. Elk and bear were often near and a moose took up residency in the willows. The cabin was nearly eighty years old. The outhouse seemed even older. A forest that covered the high mountains surrounded the green meadow. A cold creek ran nearby providing water for drinking and bathing. The smells, sights and sounds took me back to my roots. Although he was several years younger than me, we had gone to the same schools, had the same teachers and friends, and my father had been his family's attorney. He told me he had been in some trouble and went to my father for legal help. After hearing his story, my father replied, "Son, you don't need an attorney, you need a genie!" I was beginning to realize I was attracted to men with a little outlaw in them, as long as they were honest! We had hundreds of stories to share. Evenings were spent playing cards under the Coleman lantern. We drank a little whiskey, laughed, danced and became best friends. His cattle grazed the forest where we rode for hours. At the top of the mountain, we found sandstone with petrified shells and sea horses. Riding into the high mountain lakes, we camped and explored. While riding through a high mountain meadow Gary pulled up his big bay mare Keeper and reached inside an old gnarled tree. Out it came, a bottle of peppermint schnapps. I was informed that this was prime elk hunting territory and the schnapps tree always remained well stocked for Gary and his friends. Rodeos were in the same small towns where I attended rodeos since childhood. Gary was a team roper. I cheered him on. Dances at Stacy's bar were every weekend. The owners knew Buddy and me. Dad was still their attorney. Soon I felt like I'd never left home. Life was good!

Gary at schnapps tree

Gary always watched my back. One evening he didn't come home until the wee hours of the morning. I was worried. We had no telephone. I sat in the dark and worried. His whiskey tripped him through the doorway, as he stumbled in and passed out. My worry was replaced by anger. I would pack my bags and leave in the morning. When I awoke, he was gone. The small cabin door swung open. He was carrying the axe, the chopping block and a huge bouquet of Indian Paint Brush. Placing the block in the middle of the kitchen floor, he handed me the axe and the flowers, dropped to his knees and laid his head across the chopping block. Now tell me, how could you stay mad at that?

Time to paint was seldom afforded to me in Tucson. I found a watercolor artist in town. I had always painted with oils and was anxious to learn the magic of watercolor painting. Susan soon became my mentor. Life in the quiet little cabin inspired me to produce many paintings. Under the cabin

Redneck Roses

lived a family of marmots. Amazing to watch, I built them a playground from wood and rocks outside the window where I sat painting. They became gentle and ate from my hand. Gary worked construction out of town when he wasn't working on the ranch. My days alone in the little cabin watching the marmots and painting were peaceful and fulfilling, no telephone, no Sheila, no schedule, no ambulatory calls in the hot desert sun! Taking my painting to the middle of the little stream, I would sit on a mossy log submersing myself in the beauty of nature. Watercolors are amazing. One finished painting slipped into the stream and was quickly swept away. A week later it was found downstream, in a beaver pond, no worse for wear!

A small country schoolhouse a few miles away provided me a place to display and sell my art as well as give art lessons. Jackie and her blind sister Didi took my class. She was an amazing woman, having graduated valedictorian of her class at the university. She sang like an angel and had produced several recordings. After art class, I suggested we go to Stacy's for a drink. Several good old boys lined the bar, two appeared to be passed out, resting their heads on their arms. The jukebox had run out of quarters, so I asked Didi to sing a few songs. He voice, higher than first soprano, sang mostly religious songs. Her clear angelic voice rang like crystal through the bar. Being blind she was unaware of her audience and had never been in a bar before. The cowboys stared in disbelief as Didi sang on and on. One by one, they began to exit. The two asleep on the bar reared up, slid off their stools and stumbled out the backdoor. We clapped for Didi, she smiled as Jackie gave me that look again!

Summer was coming to an end, and I was scheduled to be back in Tucson to run the hospital the first week of September. Flying out of Salt Lake City, I rented a big Buick car and prepared to leave for the airport early the next morning. That night it snowed well into the morning. I had no choice but to make the long drive to Salt Lake. I had not driven in snow for years. Up the canyon toward the town of West Yellowstone I went. The snow was blinding. A large herd of Buffalo blocked the road. Carefully I wove my way through them. They looked like giant white ghosts! Although it was Labor Day weekend, I saw no other vehicles. Finally reaching the town of West Yellowstone, I turned south toward Idaho. The snow was deep on the road.

I drove the road where I had raced my dog in the sled race and memories of good times in the town of West Yellowstone flooded back to me. Semi-trucks, stuck in the storm, dotted the highway. Thankful for having a heavy car, I barreled on, passing a semi on the wrong side. I was now running three hours behind schedule! Finally the storm began to subside. I raced on, well over the speed limit. Reaching the airport, I had fifteen minutes before departure time. Leaving the car in front of the terminal I ran through the corridors and reached my destination just as the planes doors were closing. Tucson here I come!

Make my day.

26

MONTANA COMES TO TUCSON

A temperature of 110 greeted me at the Tucson airport! That was at least one hundred degrees higher than the blizzard I had driven through a few hours ago. Humidity was high from the lingering monsoon rains. They say your blood thins in high temperature to help you acclimate. September would be a difficult adjustment from the cool Montana mountains. October and November were my favorite months in Tucson and only thirty days away!

Multi-tasking was again my way of life. Operating the small and large animal hospital, ambulatory calls, showing and training my horses, teaching equine science at the community college in the evenings and continuing my art, including bronze productions, left little time for a social life. Gary came to my rescue. He fell in love with Tucson, its mild weather and western flavor, after all those cold winters of ranching in Montana. He was a good horseman and soon was training horses for my clients. We bought two-year-old colts at horse sales, then broke them to be good saddle horses. A decision was made to put on horse sales at my property. We accepted good horses for consignment, and built up a loyal clientele of consignors and buyers, several from out of state. We also established Arizona Stallion Station, leasing eight quality stallions of various breeds including one thoroughbred race stallion from France. In addition to natural breeding, we bred mares by artificial insemination from semen ordered from stallions around the world. We were spread thin but didn't stop long enough to worry about it. Gary's friends followed him to Tucson. They were team ropers and needed a climate where they could practice all winter. They lived with us. Life was crazy, never boring!

Sheila hated most men and would not call a male veterinarian or allow me to bring a male helper to her property. She was becoming crippled and was little help to me. May was having a major colic episode. Gary came along to help me. "She is going to be packing," I said "Watch for flying bullets!" She had her derringer pulled on him the minute he stepped from the truck. "Remember I divorced my husband on the grounds that he was stupid, and I don't need another stupid man on this property!" May was thrashing and crashing with pain through the mesquite. "You can't help me on those crutches. If Gary goes, I go too and you can call another vet." She never replied. Gary and I treated the old mare until she was out of pain. "I never saw a man be that gentle and good with a horse before," she explained. "What did you say his name was?" He was now her hero. "Sorry Gary, you can come here any time."

Since early childhood, Dad had taken Buddy and me to Mexico. It was a place of enchantment to us. The climate, the vegetation, the people provided us a unique experience. After leaving Washington and moving to Tucson it still intrigued me, so I shared my childhood adventures with Willie and Hallie. Shopping in Nogales or taking the train to Guymas to deep-sea fish provided relaxation and adventure for us.

Going to Mexican bars and restaurants where the gringos went was not my style. Just like Europe. I wanted to mix with the natives. In the company of a girlfriend, I found a great bar on the wrong side of the railroad tracts. The native Mexican patrons bought us tequila shots and we ate dog tacos. We would dance all night to the music provided by the mariachis. Dancing with three or four guys at the same time was crazy fun. No other women entered that bar, but the owner and patrons treated us with respect.

When Gary moved to Tucson to winter, he too was drawn to Mexico. A trip to the Sea of Cortez was a short drive from Tucson, through beautiful desert terrain. We slept on the beach, usually without a tent. A day of claming in Cholla Bay would produce hundreds of clams. The shrimp boats provided large shrimp, and the market in old town was a source of limes, garlic, butter and tequila. A fire from driftwood, a full moon, the waves pounding the sand and a seafood meal chased by a bottle of tequila created an enchanting evening. I have experienced two lunar eclipses while camping on the sandy beaches of Mexico and learned enough Spanish to interact with the Mexican people, whom I always admired and enjoyed being with. The "wetbacks" I hired for help in Tucson won my respect by their hard work and honesty. I treated them fairly and often invited them for Christmas or Thanksgiving dinner. They became loyal friends and usually returned year after year.

Gary comes to Tucson

27

BACK TO THE BIG SKY

Montana called us home the next summer. The sunsets seen from Gary's cabin blazed across the western sky. The cold stream by the cabin ran two miles to the winding, waters of the Gallatin River, a trout fishing paradise where Olympic kaykaers challenged the whitewaters. As locals, we made our rafts from four inch Styrofoam. A race with the haying crew was on. Gary and I were in the lead. Heading for the rapids, I informed him I could barely swim. Our raft flipped over. The ice-cold, green water quickly pulled me under a deeply submerged tree root toward a cold dark grave. Slowly, but surely strong arms pulled me to shore.

"Damn you woman, why didn't you tell me you couldn't swim? I lost my hat! Hat or woman was a hard decision. Might wish I'd gone for the hat. Had it longer than you. Our raft is gone, you're freezing, let's make a run for the bar. It's a mile down stream, it's getting dark and we have several barb-wire fences to get through." I was cold to the bone, never this cold before! The owners of the bar wrapped me in winter jackets and served me hot whiskey, which gradually warmed my shaking body. The haying crew arrived and named me Parnelli, after a famous British race-car driver. Like brother Bud said, "Sister, when it's your time to die, you're going to die." This was close, but not my time yet!

Montanans love their rivers. Tying a lariat to a board and then to the bridge near the bar made river surfing a challenging sport. A trip to Hawaii was not needed. The Madison River was more my speed, slow, wide and not so deep. It had provided lazy, crazy days of summer since high school. A four-hour trip in a rubber raft, pulling another raft full of beer, again provided lazy, peaceful days of summer. The Gallatin, and Madison Rivers were two of the three tributaries that form the mighty Missouri River. The third tributary is the Jefferson River, where dad and I floated and panned for gold since my early childhood. Where was Gary's sweat stained, silver belly, prized Stetson? Surely, it was floating down the Missouri by now, on its way to the mighty Mississippi! I told him that soon, a black man would be proudly wearing it in New Orleans as he boogied up Bourbon Street to Resurrection Hall. Only I thought that funny. Montana cowboys consider their hats sacred. The older, the more prized, not to be messed with. Many bar room fights resulted over abuse of a sacred hat.

I awoke to a sunny June day. It was Gary's birthday and he had already spent three hours disking the south field in hopes that he could seed his alfalfa in two to three days. The temperature was a warm seventy degrees. The Gallatin River is running high from the snow melt, but still five feet from topping House Rock in the river. We were off to Stacy's to celebrate the big day. Bloody Marys to die for with asparagus, pickles celery, beans and not too hot. I had given Gary a gold chain for his elk tooth and built

Gary

window boxes for the cabin, then painted them Irish green and planted them with poppies and geraniums.

Next we were off to an Indian friend's wedding. A large number of Indians attended. As the pretty long haired bride entered the chapel she said " Ok, you Indians can sit down now the bride is here. Then we were all back to Stacy's, standing room only, lots of Indians and lots of locals. Deno grabbed me as we entered the door, his big blue eyes shinning, he jammed me around the floor, pumping his arm like an oil derrick as he intermittently danced around the old log post that holds up the ceiling. Country Tradition sang happy birthday to Gary as every one cheered. The night melted into bliss.

Four days later it was time for round up and branding. This return trip to Montana, I could not dream of leaving Karatie so brought him with me. Climbing the steep mountain in search of cows and calves we rode through wildflower, tall, wet grass, thick stands of pine, down falls, and high mountain spring bogs. Karatie, now twenty five, traveled quickly and smoothly invigorated by the fresh mountain air, the smell of cows and the three other horses ridden by Gary, his sister and his mother. The cattle were not "bushed up" but fresh and willing to move. Gary was feeling much too cocky on his new dapple gray horse. Perhaps Karatie and I should see that he become a little more grounded. As we passed near a bog hole, I urged Karatie to side step and shouldered him to the left. Into the bog, belly deep, went Gary and his new horse. His mother looked at me in bewilderment. No one could push her son around. He was the state wrestling champion! The look she gave me was that I might die and soon. As he still struggled to free himself from the bog, I urged Karatie into a fast gallop through the forest and out of sight. We ran for a mile or so before slowing up. Finally Gary, now covered in mud, rode up behind me, his mother close behind. I decided to accept my fate and we slowed to a walk. The four letter words I expected to hear did not come. Gary leaned over from his horse, grabbed me and gave me a big kiss on the lips. How romantic was this? Now we could finish gathering the herd.

The one hundred-year-old leaning barn and corrals awaited the spring gather. The cattle entered the old holding pen and began milling around, each mother searching for her calf. More cattle were spotted on the hill to the north. Karatie quickly climbed the steep wet hill above the mavericks. He then set down on his hind quarters, pushing the remaining cattle into

the corral. Karatie was keen on cutting the calves from the cows. He snaked his neck, sometimes biting the reluctant cows. He moved through the herd with the grace of a ballerina and the determination of an Olympic athlete. This was his true love and all other interests fell to the back ground. Gary and his son roped the calves and drug them to the fire where they were branded, vaccinated, and bull calves castrated. As the old ranch had no cattle chute, the mother cows were then run into a rickety run way to be tagged with face fly repellent ear tags, receive eight way clostridial vaccinations, and to be treated with "pour on" for parasites. Young cousin Wayne, ex-bull rider accomplished these tasks by jumping from one cows back to the other as they were tightly squeezed together. Two elderly aunts leaned into the north side of the pen as it creaked and swayed in all directions. The ground crew neutralized their sore bodies with warm beer when ever the roping slowed down. An old Hereford cow with an eight inch hip abscess entered the squeeze pen. Hanging over the wooden rail I attempted to lance it with a #12 blade. As the cow jumped forward the blade went deeper. Thick white pus flew out as she burst from the squeeze corral and through the side of the near by teetering old barn. As she disappeared into the belly of the dark, straw filled creaky structure, the other cows followed her and then broke out through the plywood front door. The old barn still stood. It stood a little more hip shot, and the south wall was now missing. Out from the two story old ranch house came the cow boss, Gramma! More than a hundred years old, she was even older than the barn. Observing the leaning barn with one side missing, she shook her cane at us and let us all know she was definitely still the cow boss!

Team Ropers

Next Go Around

28

RENO OR BUST

Stringy, the bull dogger, arrived at the cabin. Dismounting his horse, he crawled through the grassy meadow picking forget-me-nots, presenting them to me with a big Italian smile. There was only one Stringy. He drove a Cadillac convertible with a set of longhorns mounted to the hood, pulling his dogging horse in a small, single horse trailer from rodeo to rodeo. His handsome features included a not-so-handsome flattened nose resulting from times he had missed his steer and plowed the arena with his face. Bar room fights added to his disfigurement. Like most Italians, he was romantic and charismatic. He tended bar at Stacy's when not on the rodeo circuit. Dancing on the bar, he imitated Elvis' gyrating movements. He was good and he knew it! The women loved him. "I came to invite you and Gary to the senior pro-rodeo finals in Reno," he said, as he handed me the bouquet of my favorite flowers. Cowboys are so romantic! Gary presented me with wildflowers on a daily basis. When he worked out of town, he always returned with a dozen white roses. "White roses signify a more special love then red roses," he explained.

Soon Stringy, Gary and I were on our way to Reno, following the longhorns on the hood. The wind blowing through my hair, the miles of Idaho and Nevada rushed by. We sang, told half-true stories, and drank beer. We were provided a deluxe room at a high roller casino. All the cowboys roomed on the top two floors. This would be a trip to remember!

Cowboys too tough to die, scarred up, tough old hides. Some were in casts and even external fixations for mending broken bones. Forty and older, some in their eighties, determined to go another round for the glory of the sport and western tradition. The halls and rooms were packed with back slapping, hand shaking reunions. Tall tales and liquor flowed up and down the top two floors of the casino. Waltzing into our room came Danny the bronc rider, behind him his girlfriend Peggy. Gary greeted them warmly, explaining to me that Danny had lost one eye when a bronc kicked him in the head. I was drinking a martini. Danny sidled over, plucked out his glass eye and dropped it into my martini. "Never be without an olive lady, little things in life count a lot. The party was in full swing. "Let's go find a bar with western dance music. Can't wait to hold my darling in my arms, Danny explained." Down to the casino floor we went. Only one bar was found and

Stringy

it wasn't western. Sitting down at a table we waited for a cocktail waitress. Swishing her skirt, she approached our table, and a deep voice asked for our order. She was very tall.

"She has such a deep, sexy voice and such long beautiful legs," gasped Danny.

"She also has an Adam's apple and I think your new love is a man, Danny," I giggled.

"No way, I'll check this matter out when she returns with our drinks."

As our drinks were placed on the table, Danny removed his glass eye, placed it under the waiter's skirt and yelled. "It has balls, it has balls!"

Within a few seconds, the bouncer had roughly escorted us out. "I think we found a gay bar. We were discriminated against because we are straight. "We have to do something to rectify this," I explained. "I have an idea. Let's go back to our rooms. The guys can wear our ladies clothes and go back in drag, we can't be thrown out then."

Watching two cowboys putting on panty hose, skirts, bras, blouses, and make up was worth the whole trip. Danny wanted to wear our friend Angie's black wig, but she would not agree to his wearing it unless he left his teeth with her as a security deposit. We were ready, Gary in my squaw dress, and Danny in Peggy's dress, sporting a long black wig and a toothless grin. Back to the bar, the drag cowboys swished their skirts, whistled at the men and asked two young men to dance. After a couple of dances, the bouncers pounced upon them. Soon we were again on the outside looking in. A Mafia appearing man approached us. "What is going on?" he asked. "I own this hotel and I don't need trouble. Are you and your girlfriends with the senior pro rodeo? See this belt buckle? I won it riding rough stock." It was the size of a hubcap and he wore it with pride, escorting us back into the bar. "Treat these folks with respect and give them all the drinks and food they want on the house!" he ordered. I snuggled up to Gary as we danced the night away, our skirts swishing too and fro. The men's restroom was outside the bar and for general public use. As Gary and Danny entered, men poured out the exit door. The night was crazy fun. Our cowboys couldn't resist going into the casino to stir up a little more excitement. I have laughed a lot in my life, but never this much. A night to remember!

Our mafia casino friend made sure we were provided a western dance every night, near the top of the casino, not far from our rooms. I believe all cowboys are born to dance. Bennie Reynolds, World Champion All-Around Cowboy from Melrose, Montana, escorted me to the floor. He was six-six, strong and sinewy. It was a fast dance.

Soon he was lifting me in the air and twirling me like a rag doll as the crowd cheered. My back surgery was still healing and another stay in traction was not desired. Gary came to my rescue.

The rodeo lasted several days. Stringy did a few face plants and also made some good catches in good time. The eighty-year-old cowboy, with the rods and pins holding his leg on, made his eight-second ride on a rough bronc! The old-timer cowboys represented nearly every state and some came from as far away as Australia. For several years, I had traveled to Las Vegas for the National Rodeos Finals, and to meet my brother Bud. Spending time together brought a flood of wonderful old memories. We enjoyed seeing the top ten young cowboys in the world ride rough stock, rope and bull-dog for seven straight days. It's a great event, but seeing the older athletes continue in their tradition in Reno was even greater!

29

FIRE IN THE HOLE!

The cabin welcomed us home. Everyone at Stacy's bar had heard about Gary's adventures in drag. Bob, the federal marshal and Gary's sidekick, had a hey day over the stories that came back from Reno. I found Bob to be a good friend. When not on duty, he enjoyed our old watering hole, as Stacy's was called. Several drinks with Bob and Hay Ray late Saturday afternoon helped me pass the time while Gary was working in Butte. I got thinking about the outhouse at the cabin. It was an old one-holer that leaned to the south. A spring ran through it and then proceeded to run toward the backdoor of the cabin, creating a swamp. "I wish I could burn that outhouse down, Bob. Let's do it while Gary's out of town. Hay Ray will help us" I exclaimed. We gathered old newspapers from the bar, trudged through the swamp, and filled the old one-holer with anything that would burn. It only smoked! Finding last year's Christmas tree, I shoved it down the hole, poured in gasoline and threw in a match. Boom! The sound echoed down the valley. Flames appeared as my helpers took my picture, proudly posing near the fire they began to sing:

She's burning the out-house down
She's burning the out-house down
She was dancing in the ashes
When we caught her with the matches
She's burning the out-house down!

As the flames were consuming most of the rickety wood frame, Gary drove home. "What are you outlaws cooking for dinner?" he asked. Caught in the act, no words were needed. The next day Bob arrived with a two-holer, probably compliments of the Forest Service. It was proudly placed down hill from the cabin.

Summer was fading into fall. Tucson was waiting. I left before the first snowflakes fell. Gary would join me after elk hunting season. We spent the next five years wintering and working in Tucson and loving our summers in Montana. Christmas in Montana became a must. Having no electricity, we could have no Christmas lights. We decorated our Christmas tree with strings of popcorn. Huge ice-cycles extended down from the steep snow packed cabin roof to the snow covered ground. "How could I give our little cabin a Christmas flare?" I wondered. The answer was easy several packages of red and green cool aid poured across the roof turned the ice-cycles bright red and green. They also made good pop-cycles. Gary's extended family made the holidays special. We hosted our annual sledding party—"Black Tie and Carhartts"—on the mountain behind the cabin. A huge bonfire, sled races, hot chili and hot-buttered rum. We all looked alike in our brown Carhartts, like a herd of elk, I thought.

MARINEL POPPIE
KENYA 1996 ©

30

AFRICA

While I was enjoying my fourth summer in Montana, Jackie had returned to Africa, busy saving the world. She and her husband were both career Peace Corps volunteers. They had spent the last ten years in Africa, and now worked with the U.S. ambassador in Kenya. "How could Jackie possibly save the world without my help?" I short-changed the time required for my immunizations, boarded a plane and before I knew it, landed in Kenya. Jackie and John lived in Nairobi in a house furnished by the ambassador. Jackie's job was to visit the small villages in the jungle and assist the villagers in obtaining aid for health services, clean water and livestock. We had an African driver who whisked us along the narrow roads in an armored truck with flags flying and horn honking. Beautiful, tall African women lined the road, carrying huge jugs of water on their heads. The first villages we entered housed about thirty people who treated Jackie like a queen. From their mud huts they retrieved two old chairs, covering Jackie's with a white lace blanket. She was queen and I a lowly princess with no lace of any color. The women and children began to dance and sing. Jackie and I joined them, dancing in and out of the jungle. We were again politely seated on our thrones, and presented with chicken dinner and a side dish. "Eat it all," she said, "or they will be terribly insulted. This is probably their only chicken, and they have so little to eat."

After the ceremonial meal, we were escorted to a deep hole in the ground. Some men were hand digging at the bottom, and sending buckets of dirt to the top with a rope. They had reached the first water and the village came alive with joy. This was our reason for visiting this little village. Jackie approved the newly hand dug well and, in their native tongue, told them she would soon deliver a submersible pump and a generator. No more long walks to retrieve safe drinking water. The people were jubilant and the dancing and singing resumed. This would be our job for the duration of my stay—helping the people who proved to help themselves. Equipment and livestock were delivered directly to the villages thus avoiding the middlemen who often misused their privileges. Yearly visits to the villages would be conducted to be certain the equipment and livestock was well cared for. We visited many villages with the intention of providing help and monitoring progress.

The natives of Kenya were a proud and striking race. Both men and women were tall and graceful. Their athletic bodies were those of distance runners and basketball players. Their children were polite and also beautiful. Jackie explained that the people of Kenya were a contrast to the natives of West Africa who were of a more muscular built. "Quarter horses versus thoroughbreds and Arabians," I thought.

We visited village after village and always were treated as royalty: Jackie the queen and I, the princess. At night we would sleep under mosquito nets, as malaria was endemic, as was cholera, typhoid, polio and AIDS. It was not unusual to see young children carrying wooden caskets on their bicycles. Road signs advertised medicine men trying to cure these diseases by bleeding out the bad blood. They then would use the same instruments on their next patients, thus spreading AIDS. A visit to an orphanage was sad, more than half of the fifty or so young children performing a structured musical for us were missing arms or legs. All were orphaned by the AIDS epidemic. Medical equipment available to them was meager, yet they happily sang and danced with beaming smiles!

Jackie and John drove me through Nairobi's national park where lions and rhinoceros still have freedom to roam. I then went to the elephant orphanage. Poaching elephants had left many orphaned young and many orphans had died at the center. It was theorized that they died because elephants have such a strong social bond. Their mothers care for them twenty-four hours a day. Feed and medical care was not enough. Around-the-clock attention was necessary for survival. Three eight-hour shifts a day, with constant play and companionship made their survival a reality. The attendants were so dedicated that rolling in the mud with the babies was part of their play. I was lucky to be included in this interaction, a treasured memory of one of nature's finest.

Boarding an old twin-engine plane, I flew 200 miles south to reach southern Kenya, northern Tanzania and the Serengeti, home to thousands of native animals. Mt. Kenya and Mt. Kilimanjaro rose to the east, thrusting their snow-capped peaks through the blue sky. Dropping altitude and crossing the Mara River, I saw what I had dreamed of—thousands of wildebeest, migrating north out of Tanzania. Beside them ran zebra, giraffe and various antelope. We were greeted at the landing strip by hundreds of aggressive baboons. A jeep ride took me to a tented camp. Jackie had warned me not to go to a Maasai village. But, after overhearing a conversation about a village several miles away, I proceeded through the

jungle in search of the Maasai. I followed a slightly worn path through brush and lush trees. Finally, there it was. I saw the entrance to a large circle of mud huts surrounded by thick, thorn-covered brush built to deter the lions from killing the livestock.

Then I saw him, dressed in his red robe, holding his spear, very tall, his skin like dark, weathered leather, his physical features like that of a high priest. He had the bearing of an aristocrat, flaunting his refinement with sensuality. As I approached, he said, "Hello, what are you doing out in the jungle by yourself?"

Without pausing, I replied, "I want to meet the Maasai because they raise and love their cattle, as do I. How did you learn such perfect English?"

"I was educated in Oxford. The eldest sons of the Maasai are sent to Europe to be educated. Follow me and I will be your host."

Looking up at this elegant man, I realized he was nearly seven-feet tall, graceful and soft-spoken. He took me to his bedroom. Inside the mud hut were two king-size beds with a fire burning between them. Lying on the first bed was a beautiful white Brahma calf.

Maasai women

"A lion killed his mother, so I keep him near to care for him. Isn't he a beauty? He will be my next herd sire. Men would kill for him!" I stroked him, his hide was soft and clean, his nose and eyes so black and gentle. "Let me escort you out to meet my family." Many small children played in front of the mud huts. Several women appeared and stared at me. Young, strong men, all dressed in red and carrying spears, gathered at the end of the compound. My new friend, the Maasai king, asked me about cattle ranching in Montana and Arizona. "I'm afraid my cattle are not so beautiful and gentle as yours. They are tough, wild mountain cattle. The ones in Arizona have some Brahma in them," I explained.

He then talked to the women in Swahili and they returned to their huts.

"I had eight wives, but one of them died of typhoid last week," he told me. "We try to vaccinate, but with no refrigeration, the vaccine is not good. We seldom eat our cows, only old or crippled cows. Our protein supply is from the blood of our cows. When taking blood, we drain it into this blood horn. My wives then cook the blood. It is very tender and nutritious and we still have a healthy cow."

"How smart is that?" I thought. "Half of the world is starving, when herein lies a simple solution!" He gifted me with a blood horn, covered with colored beads. The women emerged from their mud huts adorned in red clothing and intricate beaded jewelry. They gathered around me touching my hair and clothes. They began to sing and dance as the king looked on.

The young warriors approached, showing their athletic skills by jumping—
flat-footed—several feet in the air and throwing their spears across the
compound. This display was repeated several times. Clapping his hands, the
king signaled for the demonstration to cease. He again spoke to his seven
wives who had gathered around me. The king walked to the center of the
circle where I stood and placed a large beaded necklace around my neck. He
looked me straight in the eye, speaking to me in his native tongue. I felt very
important; I was definitely the center of attention. The king and his wives
were so kind to me and the gifts were so beautiful!

"Why did Jackie tell me not to go to the Maasai village?" I wondered.
I wore the necklace with pride as the women cheered and resumed
dancing. What a beautiful ceremony. Suddenly it dawned on me. Was this a
wedding ceremony? Did I just marry the Maasai king? Did I just replace his
dead wife?

It would soon be dark. Racing out the open gate, I ran into the jungle,
finally reaching the tented camp. Exhausted I found a table in the corner.
Still wearing the necklace and clutching the blood horn, I sank down in
my chair. The other guests of the camp were finishing their meal. A terrible
stench was in the air. It was the smell of something dead. The nearby dinner

My Maasai husband?

guest left without finishing their meal.
Something was crawling down my neck.
Maggots! My beautiful wedding necklace
was infested with maggots! Racing back
to my tent, I threw the necklace in the
corner. Was the leather backing made
from an improperly tanned cowhide? I'd
smelled a lot of dead cows. This was no
cowhide. Could it possibly be skin from
the wife who had died a few days before
from typhoid? Was this their tradition to
make a necklace from the skin of the dead
wife and gift it to the next chosen woman?
Jackie would know if I ever made it back
to Nairobi!

My wedding ceremony?

The next three days I enjoyed exploring the Serengeti in a Land Rover. There were thousands of African animals to see. A herd of cape buffalo charged our vehicle, nearly turning it over. No one invited me to join their group for our evening meals at the tent camp. I was exhausted and ready to go. My wedding necklace still lay in the corner. I poured my evening martini over it in hopes of killing the remaining maggots and terrible smell. The maggots left, but the odor remained. Wrapping it in several plastic bags, I carefully placed it in my suitcase and departed from the land of the Maasai. The Maasai cowman was not to replace my Montana cowboy!

Jackie and John shook their heads as I told them the story. When I opened my suitcase, the smell was overwhelming. The suitcase and I were escorted out of the house. My clothes and suitcase were burned. The wedding collar was hung outside on a nail and sprayed with Lysol.

Leaving my prized possession in the sun to cure, Jackie took two weeks vacation, and we headed north to climb Mount Kenya, 17,040 feet high and located on the Equator. Jackie arranged for a guide. We were only going to climb to 11,000 feet, as we had no repelling equipment. Our guide topped the scale at ninety pounds. Little but fast he was. We trudged up the mountain

Cape Buffalo

behind him. There were many fresh cattle sign. "Cape buffalo," he explained. "If they charge, you ladies, run back down the mountain. I will stay and throw rocks at them. It will be okay."

Having been told they were the most dangerous animals in Africa, and recently surviving their charge of the Land Rover, I proceeded with caution. As we continued our climb above timber-line, the trees became bushes. There was no escape if the herd detected us. The tracks became more numerous. I could smell the buffalo. "I'm out of here. Run Jackie run!" Our guide stayed behind, armed with a handful of rocks! After all that, we were awarded "Climb Mount Kenya" shirts at base camp. We were sore, tired and only wanted a good night's sleep.

Kenya has the best climate I have encountered, a year-round mild climate with light, periodic rains. I thought that living on the equator would be hot. Not so in Kenya, even in the deep jungle or on the Serengeti. Looking for the North Star on the end of the Big Dipper, I realized I was in the Southern Hemisphere where constellations unknown to me light up the night sky.

Driving across green rolling hills, we reached our next destination, Longonot Ranch, not far from Mount Kenya. Jackie had been there before. We were the only guests and were graciously greeted by African servants who also considered Jackie a queen. Six of them waited on us hand and foot. Now this was the life! The ranch was large with thousands of Brahma cattle. The living quarters were spacious, reflecting some of Queen Victoria's influence and reminding me how much of the world England had once ruled. A day of relaxation and gourmet food was greatly appreciated.

The next day found us at the stable, choosing our riding horses. All retired from the racetrack, they knew only one thing—how to run! The minute I mounted my horse, I knew that attempts to collect it and ask for various gaits would be in vain. Jackie had ridden a lot with me when we were kids in Montana. This would be different. We started toward the open range at a walk, but soon the horses broke into a lope then, grabbing their snaffle bits, broke into a dead run, flying over the hills and gullies. Zebras and giraffe joined in and antelope scattered in all directions. The horses knew nothing of neck reining or stopping. The race was on. Praying that Jackie was still behind me, my horse finally slowed to a lope, as did hers. We rode for hours, now able to enjoy the scenery and the exotic animals along our path. Stopping by a river and an outcropping of rock, we rested. It was getting dark and we had no idea how to return to the headquarters.

Headlights appeared and our African friends emerged from their vehicle, carrying a table that they placed near the high wall of rocks. A formal dining table fit for a queen was set, with candles and cocktails. My favorite of the crew proudly exclaimed he'd made the best martinis that existed just for me! The main course would challenge any four-star restaurant in the world. Dessert was served as the stars came out. We sank down in our plush chairs in the middle of what was close to heaven, sipping our after-dinner drinks. Our servants, as they called themselves, were not servants to us but good friends who treated us with respect and dignity as we treated them in return. Being in a state of bliss and total relaxation, we prepared for the long ride home. Instead we were escorted into the luxury vehicle while two of the staff mounted our tired horses and rode them back to the stable.

Reluctantly leaving Longonot Ranch, we headed west across the great Rift Valley where thousands of pink flamingos rested. To the west was Lake Victoria with its massive waterfalls. Again crossing the Rift Valley, we saw the dormant volcano Suswa, called the "Red Mountain" by the Maasai, who revere it as the sacred heart of the land. Perhaps this influenced their choice of red clothing. A Maasai man wants nothing but cows and grass: with these, thrive wives, many children and happiness. They are content with their one God Enk-ai. The tale of another god with only one son is neither credible nor welcome.

Just prior to leaving Kenya in 1996, the American Consulate was bombed by a terrorist group. The ambassador we had been working for was not injured but Jackie and John lost many friends.

I reluctantly packed to leave, but Montana was calling. Again spraying my wedding necklace with Lysol, I wrapped it and packed it for the long flight home. As I rode the escalator up to the departure floor a large advertisement of the Marlborough man was displayed. He looked just like Gary. This was a sign that it was time to go home. Arriving in Montana, I showed my wedding necklace to Gary and Bob. The smell was still overbearing and, once again, it was hung on a nail outside. Bob, being a federal marshal confirmed the skin to be human as did my friend Rob, the county coroner. I spent the next week on the tractor helping Gary mow his hay. While driving to town on an errand, I suddenly felt dizzy and hot. Pulling into a service station, I rushed to the restroom and lay on the cool tiles. I was driven to the hospital where I fought for my life for the next ten days. My body was fighting both typhoid and cholera. Montana doctors had no experience in treating either disease and, fearing I had Eboli—the most dreaded curse in Africa—they refused to enter my room and left my care to the nurses.

Brother Bud

31

LOVED ONES AND MEMORIES COVERED IN SNOW

During the time I spent with Gary, I frequently visited Dad and Bud at our nearby ranch. After being released from the hospital, I was weak and wanted to recover at Dads' house. Something was wrong. Dad was disoriented. He had Alzheimer's disease. How could such a brilliant man lose his memory? Had he worked so hard, and accomplished so much, that his neurons wore out? Brother Bud had been twice the recipient of the charge of his ton-and-a-half bull, the Red Baron, and was so crippled he could barely walk. His leg looked like it was on sideways, but he refused professional medical care. Instead, he self medicated with excessive doses of over-the-counter pain medicine, thus creating a gastric ulcer. He had always been so brave, too brave, like the time the car hit his elbow.

His veterinarian found him passed out in the pasture and rushed him to the hospital, where he was diagnosed with peritonitis and multiple organ failure from a perforated stomach ulcer. Bud lay in a coma for days, never to see me again. I wanted to tell him how much I loved him, but he couldn't hear me. His doctor was my high school classmate, and I knew he would save him if at all possible. I took Dad to see him twice daily. Dad seemed so confused and so sad. After ten days of hoping and praying, Bud's life-support system was turned off. Only in his fifties, my big brother, my special, special friend was gone.

Dad continued to deteriorate. His eyes developed a faraway look, yet they never lost their twinkle. Daily I took him to the park, the museum, fishing, or to see his friends. He never was mean. I told him stories about the past. He told me his favorite memory on several occasions. "Remember Sister when I climbed over the mountain and saw the cowboys with guns and the wolf howled in the night?" then dad would howl, a long mournful howl. Memories of being a Navy courier who hand-delivered messages to the world's top leaders at the first United Nations meeting meant nothing to him now. They never had. I took him to Gary's little cabin and he asked, "Sister, where is the other half?" He had not lost his sense of humor! We invited thirty of his friends for a dinner party. To my amazement, he understood they were coming, and dressed in his finest suit. He greeted his guests at the door, knowing each by name. He was the perfect host as being a gentleman could not be taken from him by any disease. Until his last day, he always

opened doors for the ladies, and politely sat them at the table. Dad's wife placed him in a lock-down retirement home. She had loved him so much, that she drank day and night to ease the pain. She became yellow, bloated, and whiskey mean. She died that summer, not long after I lost Bud.

Summer was fading into winter. I could not dream of leaving Dad alone in the Montana rest home. Gary agreed to help me take him to Tucson. Gary had helped me through all these sad ordeals, always watching my back. Our cattle and beautiful ranch had to be sold. Nothing left of nothing was again evident. My wonderful, wonderful memories, left behind, to be covered by a blanket of snow.

32

ADVENTURES WITH DAD IN TUCSON

Tucson greeted Dad, Gary and me with a blast of hot, humid air. Gary offered to watch Dad full time, so I could continue to work the vet practice and all my other multi-tasking. He had always respected and admired Dad and Dad liked Gary. Dad got a twinkle in his eye when he saw Gary's mother. "Maybe we're half brother and sister?" I joked to Gary. "Our parents were both stationed at the same naval base at the same time. I have seen your mother smile at dad in a special way. No wonder we have so much in common."

When Dad got restless, Gary would drive him around and around the block, much to Dad's delight. My many pets helped keep him content too. If he had a bad moment, we'd put on our cowboy hats and sing together. Frequent visits to the veterinary clinic caused some apprehension when Dad would try to run off with the client's pets. I had no doubt where my connection to the animal kingdom came from.

Afraid Dad might fall into the swimming pool in the court-yard we built a six-foot wall around the front of the house. Dad would be safe there and could work in the little garden we'd made for him. Shortly after the wall was built, we showed Dad the garden and went inside the house. "He'll be happy and safe now. He loves to be outside," I told Gary. Seconds later, Dad scaled the wall like a monkey, and ran over to the vet clinic where Truly Nolan's termite exterminating mouse mobile was parked. The Volkswagen, with tail, ears, and a rodent's smiling face was well known in Tucson. Into the "mouse-mobile" climbed Dad, turned the key and raced out the gate yelling, "I'm going back to Montana!" After a long chase through traffic, he was finally stopped. He wouldn't get out until Gary yelled, "Come on, let's go drink some whiskey and chase pretty girls! I have your cowboy hat." Dad bolted from the mouse mobile and we were on the way to the Cow Pony. The bartender knew to dilute Dad's drinks as we toasted Montana and had a great time.

A pacemaker would be needed. Surgery was scheduled. Only two pretty nurses could insure their wary patient would be admitted and placed in a room. He repeatedly tried to leave. Gary and I slept on cots in front of his door blocking his escape. It was a long, long night and surgery was scheduled early the next morning. He refused a wheelchair, so we walked him down the long corridor and into the operating room. Dad was dumb like a fox. He smelled a rat. When the anesthesiologist approached, Dad took him out with a Montana punch, and then went after the doctor who jumped on top of the surgery table to escape. Gary was trying to hold the door shut, but was knocked out of the way as Dad ran up the hall in his hospital gown, barn door a-flapping.

I never knew Dad was so strong. Gary had been state wrestling champion and won most of his barroom brawls, but he was no match for my dad with a failing heart! Plans were made to attempt surgery again the next morning. Again we slept on cots to block the door during the night. A mild sedative was given to Dad. Gary and I had retrieved the three black cowboy hats. We all wore them that night, singing cowboy songs. Again a wheelchair was refused, so off we went for the second time, down the long corridors, through the crowded waiting room and toward surgery. The three musketeers in black hats, with the surgery candidate in the center, barn door again flapping, proudly wearing his black hat. Again he smelled a rat! A large family of Mexicans visited in a room we passed. Grabbing a baby from a woman's arms, Dad dove into the room and hid in the crowd of startled Mexicans. Dad had always loved babies and was handling the infant with care. Explaining the situation to the child's mother, she retrieved her infant and asked Dad to follow her and the baby up the hall. Dad went along and we were almost there but he bolted again when he saw the large doors leading to surgery. I shoved a large food cart in front of him to block his retreat. The woman with the baby walked into the surgery room and the heart surgery patient followed. Gary again barred the door. The doctors and nurses hid behind a partition. An anesthesiologist appeared. I hoped he had a dart gun. As Dad fought to exit the door, the anesthesiologist injected him from behind. Two large orderlies placed him on the surgery table, the doctors and nurses emerged and the lady and her baby left with us. We graciously thanked her and went home. Dad was to stay in recovery for two days. Six hours later we received a call. He was last seen running down the hall. Would we please come get him? I realized, I had never seen my father sick or in need of medical care before. He was a tough old bird!

Once back home, Dad became frightened of bathing. Gary suffered two black eyes while trying to convince him a shower was good. We had no choice but to place him in a home. He lasted two days in the first home and one day in the second. We went to his rescue as he stood on a porch, suitcase in hand, looking sad and confused. Finally I found a facility with an arboretum in the center. He seemed to like it there, as he could see the trees and flowers. They had a special setup for bathing. It sounded like a cattle chute to me, but it worked. They explained that he would not be allowed in the arboretum when the temperatures in Tucson reached seventy degrees. But on one of my daily visits, I found him, in his black sweat suit, passed out in the arboretum. He had suffered a heat stroke. The temperature was over 100 degrees and they had not locked the area. He slowly deteriorated after that. He didn't seem to know my name, but was always happy to see me. On Father's Day, June 17, 2000, Dad was ninety-one years old. I received a call saying his color was not good, but he was okay. Gary and I rushed to see him. An employee held an oxygen mask over his nose. There was no oxygen left in the tank! They were suffocating him and his fingers were turning blue. "You idiot, there's no oxygen in this tank," Gary yelled as he knocked the employee over and ran for a new tank. Dad responded and his fingers regained their color. He was weak. I gave him his Father's Day card and snuggled up to him. Two hours later, his respiration slowed and he peacefully drifted out of my world. They came to get him, but I couldn't let go. They pried him out of my arms. I wanted to go with him. I felt like I was drowning, as the tears wouldn't stop. I knew he was saying, "Cow Girls Don't Cry."

Reaching home, I climbed bareback on Karatie and raced blindly through the desert. Thunder and lightning broke through the evening sky. Rain fell with intensity, as the storm increased from a sky like I had never seen before. Fast-moving clouds with colors of the sunset raced around heaven. Suddenly the clouds parted, long streaks of silver light broke through. It was as though the heavens had opened up to take my father home.

I took Dad back to Montana. Many friends paid their respects at the stately pine-covered cemetery. The military gun salute echoed across the green valley, as he was placed in the ground in our family plot. It is a peaceful place where in summer green grass carpets the earth beneath tall pines, to be replaced in winter by a carpet of snow that sparkles like diamonds. A place where Magpies fly and where I jumped my stallion, Hitan, over my grandfather's and grandmother's gravestones . . . a place where I will later join them . . . a place where heaven meets Montana.

33

OVER THE MOUNTAIN
TO THE LAND OF ENCHANTMENT

Tucson had treated me well. For thirty-four years it provided many friends, a challenging, successful, veterinary practice, many adventures and beautiful memories. However, the work-load at the veterinary clinic, equine surgical center, and breeding barns increased to the point that, one day, I realized I didn't even have time to pet my own dogs. Every minute, it seemed, I was caring for other peoples' animals. I no longer had time for my art and little time to ride my horses for pleasure. Having undergone multiple orthopedic surgeries, the granite-hard tile floors of my home and hospital were a constant reminder of my rearranged body parts.

Loving the ranching lifestyle, Gary and I decided to find a ranch in the Southwest and sell the home, hospital and stallion station in Tucson. Southwest New Mexico was beautiful and had a 20,000-acre ranch for sale just east of the Arizona border. The ranch was high, rugged, and surrounded by forest. It would experience the four seasons, but winters would not be severe. Cattle would not need to be fed hay since the land provided feed year-round. Everyday I could ride my horses, interacting with my dogs, while taking care of the herd.

Gary and I married in Montana on the mountain behind his cabin. More than a hundred guests were there. We danced in the meadow until morning. We then said goodbye to Montana and left to begin our new life in New Mexico.

Wedding guests (top); the ranch (bottom)

34

A STEP BACK IN TIME

The ranch's only building was a very old, tumbled down line shack where local historians say Butch Cassidy, the Sundance Kid, and possibly Billy the Kid, hung out after their robberies. Only five miles from the Arizona border, they could escape the law with a fast ride to the west. The Mollogon Rim stretches from Arizona to this unpopulated area. A ghost town remains twenty miles up the rim from the ranch. It was once a thriving mining town where cowboys, miners and liquor ran free. Apache Indians wars were prevalent. Artifacts of their presence are commonly found, as are those of the Anasazi Indians who mysteriously disappeared 2,000 years earlier leaving black and white pottery of a quality unequaled in the world. A small town of roughly 250 people lies nestled in the valley below. A stream shaded by numerous trees wanders through town, thus it is called Glenwood. Its people are friendly and non-materialistic. It has one mom-and-pop grocery store, gas station, three churches, a restaurant and two bars. The ranch and small town are contained within the boundary of Catron County. Though it is one of the largest counties in the United States, less than 4,000 people

Wild horses

make up the population, mostly ranchers and loggers. Directly east of the
ranch, lies the rugged Gila National Forest and Wilderness area. The Apache
Indian reservation and the Blue primitive area are to the west. To the north,
the great plains of St. Augustine stretch for miles toward the Rio Grande
River. Few people, but thousands of antelope inhabit these vast plains.
People of Catron County are known to take care of their own problems.
Most residents carry guns. The slogan for Catron County is "shoot, shovel
and shut up!"

   Our ranch home is located ten miles from town. No other residents
occupy this mountain. Gary rebuilt the old outlaw hangout with flagstone
and knotty pine. He saved the old doors that had once welcomed desperate
men. Our new home would be even smaller than his cabin in Montana. We
slept on the floor, and ate outside by the campfire.

   I bought 350 head of wild, rock-footed Braford cattle from Arizona.
They'd been gathered from the mountains between Tucson and the Mexican
border. When they arrived, Gary said, "those cows don't have horns, they
have antlers." They were wild, unlike the gentle, purebred cattle raised on
irrigated pastures in Montana. Because I had spent time in Africa, it was
rumored they were African watuzi cattle. These cattle were survivors!

They needed no special care, as they knew how to find water and had no trouble calving. They didn't like people and, when corralled, were defensive and dangerous. If on foot, we were quickly put over the fence. When on horseback, our horses were often knocked out from under us. It was time to cowgirl up! Karatie, now in his thirties, was my best mount. He would attack the charging cattle. Adrenaline rushed through both of us. The seven other horses I bought from Tucson, were turned out on the 20,000 acres of forest land to learn how to be real horses, leaving their box stalls behind. Gary chose our brand to be a rocking arrow on the left shoulder. Our business would be Rocking Arrow Cattle Company.

One day we found a maverick bull. He was about two years old with horns, black in color with a little brown tiger striping. After considerable effort we were able to run him off the mountain and into the corral. As soon as we followed him into the corral he charged both of our horses, knocking my mare out from under me then turning to charge Gary's horse. He was relentless in his pursuit injuring both horses. I ran to get my new little tractor, which he also repeatedly charged. Gary finally roped his hind legs and managed to dally them around a post. As the bull tried to attack me on the tractor seat, I got a rope around his horns and pulled him through the corral and into the next corral with the tractor. We had him stretched out so far he looked like a dachshund. We then proceeded to brand, vaccinate and castrate him. The horses were beat up, we were beat up, the tractor was

Painting by author

dented and the young bull was still on the hook after being released. The next morning I walked to the corral to see if he was OK. He should have settled down by now. He wasn't in the corral where we had left him. He had hidden behind the barn. Suddenly he charged, hitting me so hard, that I was thrown twenty feet into a pile of rocks, where he ground me into the rocks with repeated blows. My dogs tried to save me but this only made him madder. He was in a blind rage. Finally as he turned his rage on the dogs, I was able to roll under the fence to safety. Multiple bruises, several broken ribs and a broken collarbone reminded me of my encounter with the "Shaq". Thus I had named him after my friend Shaquille O'Neal, big, dark and very athletic.

Gary did a great job of restoring the old outlaw shack. He had his hands full and I had no choice but to continue work in Tucson, as we would have little money until the Tucson property sold. Although younger than me, Gary suffered a severe stroke. We had only been married for one year. His family came down from Montana and took him home. This was probably his only chance to heal and I was left alone. Finally, my clinic and property sold. I was free to live in New Mexico, free to run the ranch! I was so lonely and knew my sole survival would be a challenge. Like Dad always told me, buck up, cowgirls don't cry!

35

WHERE HAVE ALL
THE FLOWERS GONE?

When I bought the ranch, it was lush and green—like Ireland, I thought. The winter brought good rains before I purchased the cattle. The rains seemed to never come again. The grass turned brown and curled into the ground. Nearly all of the forty-three dirt water tanks went dry. My home was five miles up the mountain from the river to the east and five miles down the mountain from the Arizona state line to the west. My home was the only building on the mountain. I was truly alone. The cattle began to starve. Many would die as I tried to drive them down to the house and corrals. Hay, nearly impossible to find, would be impossible to haul up the rugged mountain to the cattle. The native ranchers said they had never seen anything like it.

By mid summer, I had thirty orphaned calves to bottle feed each day. One calf was extra special. His gray, Brahma mother had made it off the mountain only to collapse in the corral. I gave her IV fluids and glucose for two days. Her head and giant horns rested in my lap as she took her

last breath. I had named her Princess. "You better haul her to the dead cow area," I said to the hired man on the tractor. He was stopped as he started to pull her away, "Wait, she is having a calf!" I yelled. A beautiful big, white Brahma calf, much like the one on the Maasai king's bed emerged. Princess had saved all her remaining strength to reproduce. Within a few minutes he was standing and looking at me with beautiful dark eyes. I named him Peek-A-Boo. We bonded like a mother and her calf. He followed me everywhere, including into the house. He became my symbol for survival. If he could make it, so could I.

Self portrait with Karatie

36

TALK OF THE TOWN

When you're new to an area, and don't know anyone, it's nice to put your best foot forward. I put both left feet forward. The brand inspector was coming to confirm that my brand was on a cow that had jumped the cattle guard and run off to a neighboring ranch. I wanted to make a good impression when he arrived. My horse was saddled; I only needed to snap my bat-winged chaps. I snapped them all right, the right leg to the left leg. Unknowing that I had hobbled my legs together I introduced myself while shaking the brand inspector's hand. Attempting to mount my horse, I fell flat on my back! What could I say as I lay looking up at him? Of course he also owned the local tavern where the story of the new gal in town quickly circulated.

Because of the drought, I was forced to haul the cattle to high-timbered country where snowmelt had left enough moisture for some grass. The area was sixty miles from the ranch up a narrow, winding road called the Bursum Road. It wound through the Mollogon ghost town and then upward for another thirty miles, where the canyon walls kissed the front bumper as you made the sharp turns. The trailer could haul up to nine big cows or six cows with calves. My ranch hand Fred and I made so many trips, and still had more than 100 cows and calves to move. I had purchased a new Chevy diesel, three-quarter-ton pickup truck. Having acquired a spa for the new addition to the house, I examined the large cardboard carton it was packed in.

"Fred," I began, "let's put this shipping container in the back seat and use it to haul the calves, then we can always haul nine cows. This will reduce the number of hauls we make by a third."

"Great idea" he replied, "just like a cop car." So off went Fred, nine cows in the trailer and nine calves in the back seat. An hour later I got a call from him. "What's up?" I asked.

"Your new truck quit on the sharpest, narrowest turn possible. Traffic from the ghost town is backed up in both directions. I hiked three miles down the mountain so I could call you."

"The truck is brand new and I filled it with gas last night"

"You filled it with gas? It's a diesel, no wonder it stopped! You better see if you can get a wrecker from Silver City. My friend Jim is coming with his stock trailer to unload the cows, but is will be impossible to unload the calves. I have a sheer rock wall on the right side and a thousand foot drop off on the left."

The Chevy garage agreed to send a wrecker. "Don't worry lady, we will haul your truck to Silver City, find out why it quit, fix it and even detail it for you. It's brand new and under warranty. We take pride in our customer service."

"Detail it," I thought, if they only knew!"

Four hours later a wrecker arrived and hauled the truck and nine bawling calves to the bottom of the mountain where they could be unloaded. What a mess! The cardboard was soaking wet and torn to shreds. Manure and urine covered the seat, windows, door -panels and ran down into the electronic window controls.

"Never seen anything like it. Never. No, never!" exclaimed the tow truck driver as he stared at me. Gathering my courage, I called the Chevy garage the next day. "Lady you put gas in your diesel tank, but considering the circumstances we are going to report it as an electrical problem so your warranty will cover all the expenses."

Arriving to get my truck, I was informed it was good as new, but the detail man was not too happy. He emerged from the back room, a young buck wearing an old black western hat. "A little cow shit never bothered me!" he said

Building a fence

37

THE HIGH COUNTRY

Soon after the cattle were hauled to the high country, a wild fire blew through and ran some of the cows into the Gila Wilderness. Fred and I rode in search of them. After riding for eight hours, we reached a swampy stream. Smokey crossed with Fred, but my little mare, Sky, having just arrived from Tucson, had not seen water before except in a bucket. When I asked her to cross, she bolted sideways, falling over a large log. Pinned beneath her, my right side was crushed. She couldn't regain her footing as her legs were splayed over the large fallen tree. Fred came to my rescue. For forty-five minutes, he pulled up on her saddle horn and inched me out by my shoulders. She lay still until I was finally freed. Pulling me away from her, Fred rolled her off the log. She scrambled to her feet, with multiple cuts. The Spam cans in the right saddlebag were oozing down the saddle-bag and the horse after being crushing and spilling much of our weeks rations. My leg could bear weight, so I knew it wasn't broken. I was bruised to the bone, from my toes to the top of my head. I felt like the smashed Spam. Fred wanted to take me to the hospital, but we had a job to do and I insisted we go on.

We rode until dark to make camp. The next morning I was purple and green. I mounted Sky with Fred's help and we rode on, meeting a bear on the high trail the first ten minutes out of camp. We rode for seven days and found no cattle or cattle tracks, only tracks of elk, deer and wolf. No other humans were seen. Finally reaching home, a soft bed and pain medicine began my healing process.

The high country suddenly turned cold. We loaded the cattle and made numerous trips down the steep rugged mountain road to the ranch. Finally, we were hauling our last load. Nine large cows were in my twenty-four foot stock trailer. Fred followed with their calves pulling a second trailer. A snow had fallen that morning. By afternoon it had turned to black ice. Pulling my load up a hill, the tires began to spin. The trailer full of cows was sliding backward toward a thousand-foot shale cliff. Nothing I did would stop the backward descent. With only seconds to spare, Fred slammed his truck into my trailer, knocking it into the uphill ditch. Too scared to move, I slumped over the steering wheel. When Fred opened the door and helped me out, we both fell on the black ice. Finally reaching the ranch, a head count revealed we had lost a third of the original herd to the drought and the fire. Eventually the late summer monsoons brought the rains. Once again, the grass and flowers emerged from the summer's parched earth. The ranch and I had barely survived our first year and our first drought. The cattle and I began to recover. The next eight years were drought free and we had work to do.

Many of the dirt tanks that caught the summer and winter rains were breached. A bulldozer was used to repair the dams. Corrals and fences were sixty-years-old and in need of repair. Fred was strong, like a bull, and could climb the mountains like a grizzly. We built long expansions of new fence through the forest. Unlike the treated pine fence posts in Montana that were pounded into the ground by a tractor, we cut fence posts from juniper trees as we made our way up through the forest. Limbs from the trees were used as stays to fill the space between the posts. Post-holes were dug by hand through the rocky soil. I learned the rocky ground was a blessing, as it stopped erosion and held the moisture. We built fence summer and winter.

The horses learned to cover the rocky ground with agility. They quickly developed a lot of cow sense. Sorting cattle in the corral seemed natural to them. This ranch could not be managed without good horses. Roads were not an option given the rugged terrain. ATV's were useful only to haul salt, not to gather cattle.

38

INTRODUCTION TO BANNANA HORNS

The cattle I had grown up with in Montana were gentle, irrigated pasture cattle. I was certain Dad had cattle just so I could drive them with my horse. They were fat, slow and often needed help calving. You could look across the flat pastures and actually count your cows.

The wild cattle of New Mexico are elusive, athletic survivors. People say "dumb old cows." Not so. They intrigue me with their intelligence. I study their behavior and survival skills, engaging in a constant awareness of their environment, including feed, water and predators.

Having barely survived my first year ranching during the drought, I am determined to make up for cattle lost and insure success for the ranch in the future. It has become clear that nature will always be in control. My success depends on working with her. I've learned from my many mistakes. My life revolves around my environment and the cattle. In fact, I have begun to think like a cow, but it takes a cow to know a cow. So listen to their story, as told by Banana Horns, and you'll gain an understanding of ranch life in the Southwest.

•••••

Hello, my name is Banana Horns. For a long time I lived in a deep canyon in New Mexico with five other cows and their calves. How I got here, I am not sure. I do remember clanging gates and loud and fast shouting as I was run through a small corral. Loaded into a big, noisy truck, with other cows, I traveled for miles. Finally I was run down a steep chute and turned out into wild, rocky country. I had never seen open range before, only my small pasture where I was fed hay. Possibly I was a 4-H project. If so, I am sure I won no blue ribbon, as I am not elegant and have only small 'banana horns' loosely hanging from my head.

Two months ago, people riding horses entered the canyon. Seeing the horses and riders the cows threw up their heads and began to run. Not wanting to be left behind, I followed. One rider said, "these cattle are the cattle we've been hunting for the last three years." They followed behind us, softly whistling. Two cows ran up the mountain. A rider raced ahead of them, turning them back to the herd.

We were driven into a large wooden corral. There were about 100 cows in the next corral. I had not seen these cows before. Many were agitated, hooking each other with their horns. The calves were of all sizes. My heifer calf was almost as big as me. She was still nursing. She was a good calf. Dancer, a gray cow, had been driven to the corral once every year for the last five years. There her calf was taken from her. The people on the horses were called cowboys and one, a cowgirl. I heard one of the cowboys say, "that skinny black cow has banana horns just like some of the bulls we ride at the rodeos." Some of my friends were beautiful cows. Most of them were fat and slick with huge horns. Someone said, "These cows look like they have antlers, their horns are so big." His friend answered, "That's the type of cattle we need in this rough country so the cows can protect their calves from predators like coyotes, wolves, bears and mountain lions." The cows with pretty horns were like homecoming queens. They moved through the corral with ease, heads held high, as the polled cows with no horns stayed their distance. I found a corner where my calf and I could feel a little safer. Peek-A-Boo stayed between the herd and us. He seemed to know we needed protection. We all felt free and happy out on the range. I'd never seen the cows be aggressive toward each other. The horned cows did, however run in little cliques of six to ten, showing mutual respect and confidence.

A red cow with a white mottled face raced up and down the corral. She had one long horn and one had been broken off. Suddenly, she jumped not one, but three tall wooden fences and ran into the canyon. She had cleared

those fences like an Olympic high jumper so the cowboys had named her Jumper. Suddenly, she came racing back, as she had left her calf behind. The ranch hands roped, branded, ear tagged and vaccinated her calf then turned it out to join her.

Two riders rode into the corral to sort the cattle into various groups. The horse's job was to cut or separate the cows. Bulls were turned out, as they were fighting and damaging the old wooden fence. Unbranded calves and calves to be weaned were separated from the cows. Thin cows or cows in need of medical attention were driven into a treatment corral. Some cows were thin due to nursing big calves or because they were old and did not have enough teeth to forage. Cows, unlike horses have only bottom teeth in the front part of our mouth. After these wear out we cannot eat and can die of starvation. Most of the cows are a hardy Brahma cross. If they still had good teeth, they were turned out for another year to raise another calf. I overheard the ranch owner say, "I hate to sell the 'broken mouthed' cows, but it's sad to find one that starved to death because I did not sell her in time. This range is too rough for cows will poor teeth!"

Calves were roped, then branded, ear tagged and vaccinated. Male calves were castrated. Later, small calves were turned out with their mothers. It is

Branding the calves

Branding the calves (left), and cowboy, veterinarian and friend Doc. Bill Anters (right)

important cows and calves "pair up" together before being turned back on to the range, as disoriented calves could fall prey to predators. The brands would be a deterrent to rustlers. Calves weighing 450 pounds or more and "short weight" calves with thin mothers were taken to the weaning pasture. Newly branded calves could not be taken to the sale yard for three weeks, until their brands peeled. I watched this process from the corner where I stood with my calf. Some cows ran the cowboys over the fence. One cow knocked down the horse the cowboy was riding. You could feel the adrenaline in the air from the cows and the horses and riders. Dancer, a blue roan, part milk cow was standing near me. I think she's the smartest cow on the ranch. She loved her calves and had raised not only her own calf during the hundred-year drought five years ago but, on her own, adopted three orphaned calves. I wondered where Dancer got her name. Miss Fitzgerald, an old but wise Brahma cow, told me the story. One day a ranch hand, without a horse, tried to load Dancer into the stock trailer. Now, Dancer did not want to go on the bus ride. The man was big and strong, but Dancer had him on the run. Two railroad ties stood solitary in the corral. He ran figure eights around the railroad ties to avoid the cow, who had no horns but a lot of savvy. Finally, tired of the chase, he turned and grabbed Dancer by both ears, dragging her up the alley way and into the stock trailer. The corral dance was one to remember and thus Dancer got her name!

Now Miss Fitzgerald, named by the ranch owner, got her name because she reminded the owner of her seventh-grade principal. She was tall and sort of pear-shaped. She had long crooked legs, a long face with freckles and big brown glasses. She proudly wore a magnificent set of three-foot horns making her extremely authoritative. She was brown tiger-stripe in color, much like the first Miss Fitzgerald's' pinstripe suits. Though fifteen years old, she was fat and slick and produced a big healthy calf every year. She ruled with authority but fairness. The other cows respected and seemed to like her.

The neighboring corral was empty after separating the cows, calves and bulls. We were moved into that corral and the same process of sorting began. I was so thin that I was quickly separated from my year-old heifer and put into the fatten-and-sell lot with other thin or old cows. My beautiful heifer was loaded into the stock trailer with the other large and branded calves and taken to a weaning pasture several miles away. Range cows are good mothers and if separated from our calves we'll go through miles of pastures and fences to find them. A cow will always return to the last place she saw her calf. Weaning time is hard. Our bags continue to fill with milk for several days, but weaning is essential so we can prepare for our next calf.

Ruby Red, a magnificent red, tiger-striped Brahma-cross cow, calved on the mesa. She had a strong and playful black calf. When he was only a few days old, a mountain lion killed him. Ruby had big horns and was very wise, but no match for the lion that killed her calf, ate its heart and lungs and then moved on. Ruby stood over the little black body day after day. The coyotes and crows tried to rob her of her dead calf. They came at her from all directions, but she would not let them take him. Her milk bag became so large I thought it would break. Still Ruby stood guard over the lifeless little body. She did not eat or drink for days. A group of coyotes, circling the dead calf, finally dragged it down into the steep canyon. Ruby gave up hope and joined the herd. I learned the big cat was probably a tom as he only made that one kill and then moved on. That's what males often do but a mother mountain lion will bury the carcasses under leaves and return to train her kittens to hunt.

Range cows have a lot of room. We stay in small groups, often ten or less. This helps us keep diseases and parasites away. When cows calf, some leave the herd, others prefer to stay nearby. Standing in a circle around a cow that is calving, we protect her. Mother cows usually lose weight the first week after calving. After a few days, we leave our calf with a babysitter cow during the day in to consume enough feed to produce milk. We rotate turns for babysitting. The babysitter may have as many as ten calves to watch over. Mother cows come back to nurse their calves several times a day. As the calves are born, the mothers with the same age calves tend to group together. Who is selected to be babysitter of the day, is a mystery known only to cows. Though I am small with banana horns, I produce good calves. Living on this rugged range has made me strong and wise. After my big heifer was weaned, I put on weight and was turned back into the herd.

•••••

39

DIRT TANKS

Gestation for cows is nine months. Calves are ideally weaned and sold in the fall at nine months of age. After a cow calves, she normally will breed back by sixty days. Calves in northern states like Montana, ideally, are sold in the fall before the winter becomes severe, thus preventing the need for winter feed. Northern cows must therefore, calf by February to produce calves that will be weaned and sold in the fall. Calving in the freezing winter is a full-time job for the northern rancher. Calves born in the cold often freeze, so herds require monitoring day and night. My brother Bud slept with the herd during the freezing winters to watch over the calving. Because southwest winters are milder, ranchers don't have to worry about synchronized breeding and calving. The first 350 cows I purchased were "three-stripers"—carrying calves into the third trimester, thus to uniformly calf in the spring. The droughts have disrupted all this. Many cows have reabsorbed their calves, saving their strength for their own survival. Everything is thrown off schedule. Pulling the bulls and waiting a year to breed the cows back would be the only answer to again producing uniform calf crops. If I could manage to gather all my bulls, bulls from neighboring ranches would replace them. Nature knows best. The droughts have caused most cows to calf in the summer, rather than the spring, because summer rains produce the best feed. I am grateful for a healthy calf, born any time of the year. When the dirt tanks are full and the grass is good, life is good for both my cows and me.

As the dirt tanks dry up they become dangerous mud suck holes. Cattle smelling the little remaining water wade into the death traps for a last drink. Their heavy bodies sink down to their backs in the heavy mud. When found their heads are often the only part of their body not submerged. Saving them is difficult. Trying to rope them from the shore is rarely successful, thus it requires wading up to your waist or higher through the mud to place a rope around their head. They are often thrashing in a state of panic, thus dangerously knocking you around. If it is a horned cow, placing the rope is easier than going over the head to the neck. I often feel trapped by the cold sucking mud and realize I could die there with the cow. If the dirt tank is near a road, the back-hoe can pick the cow up and drag her to dry land after the ropes have been placed on her head. If not, my ATV will sometimes have enough power to drag her to safety. A horse can sometimes pull the cow to shore, but it feels like the chinch will break as the horse scrambles to free the cow. I purchased a 1951 World War II power wagon this year that can climb the rough terrain and hopefully pull the cows out by means of a winch. After the cows are drug to shore, many of them have given up and refuse to stand. I have spent weeks hauling hay, water and drugs to these poor "downer" cows. After many years of facing this situation I have learned that if a cow does not stand by the third day, I must shoot her to put her out of her misery.

Cleaning the silt from these dirt tanks with a bull-dozer is helpful. Care must be given to remove only the silt and not break the clay barrier which gives the bottom of the tank stability. One heavy rain may again refill the tanks with silt, making cleaning of the forty-three dirt tanks nearly impossible. The dirt tanks are therefore a blessing and a curse.

Seldom able to gather a hundred calves of weaning weight at the same time, I usually don't have enough calves to fill a semi-truck. Therefore, I haul twenty-five calves to the sale yard at a time in my twenty-four-foot stock trailer. The sale yard is five hours away. I pray for no flat tires but that prayer is not always answered. Trip after trip, it seems there's always that last lug nut I can't loosen when I get a flat tire. It's 106 degrees, the stock trailer is full and I can't change the flat tire. The tar in the asphalt melts, sticking to my boots and Levis. Of course, the flat is on the south side of the trailer, not in the shade. No one will stop and I am in the middle of nowhere. Knowing I have to get these cattle to the sale yard before the heat does us all in, I proceed with only three good tires to a town forty miles away. The tire looks like it has an afro when I pull into a station to get it changed. On my way again, I have fifty more miles to go. Once on the interstate, semi-trucks whiz by. I have only twelve more miles to go. Smoke begins to billow up from the right rear trailer tire. The wheel bearing is going. It's happened several times before. Stopping is not an option on the busy interstate. I put the pedal to the metal and race on, hoping to reach the sale yard before the trailer catches fire. Just as I reach the unloading dock, the flaming tire and wheel fly off across the stock-yard. Yells erupt from every direction as Mexican cowboys run toward the flames, dousing the wheel with water. I made a grand entrance, but at least I made it!

Lucky to find a mechanic who could replace the wheel, I make a quick stop to buy groceries and head back home, this time on the freeway, not the winding, narrow mountain pass. Boom! Oh no, not another flat tire. Sure enough, and I can't turn the last lug nut. A National Guard convoy is stopped on the freeway. Running across the median, I persuade them to come to my rescue. On down the highway I continue. I only have a hundred miles left to go. Boom! "Not again!" Stepping out on the hot sticky asphalt, I search for the flat tire. The tires look okay. I'm getting paranoid. I continue the drive home. Twenty minutes later, there's another loud boom and, again, I find no flat. I can't believe it. Am I so hot and tired that I'm hallucinating? Dragging myself back into my truck, I see two soft, white forms dangling above the back seat. "What is that on the ceiling?" I wonder. "Is that dough?" The biscuits I'd bought from the grocery store have exploded in the intense heat! Slumping down behind the steering wheel, I laugh long and hard before the long trip home.

40

A SIGN FROM LESLIE

I have always liked bears. In the ten years of working this ranch before this terrible drought, I have only seen two bears, and have not known them to kill adult cattle. Three years ago, I lost a dear friend to bone cancer, beautiful blue eyed Leslie. We had been close friends since our high school ski racing days. Leslie loved bears, so I gave her bear jewelry, figurines and books. She used to be part of the group that went to the West Yellowstone dump to drink beer and watch the bears. For six years she fought her bone cancer. The day she lost her battle drove me into a deep depression. I drove my ATV up the mountain to the highest pasture. Just as I topped the hill, a darling cinnamon-colored cub rolled off the hill in front of me, then lumbered down into the canyon. This was the first bear I'd seen in seven years of working the ranch and I am outside eighty-percent of each day. To me this was a sign from Leslie! An hour later, I headed down the mountain. To my amazement, a huge black bear crossed the road in front of me. He stood still looking at me for a long time, before slowly walking into the timber. Another sign from Leslie! I knew she had gone to a better place. The night sky at the ranch is bright with millions of stars. I look at the constellation Ursa Major and hold my fond memories of adventures with Leslie close to my heart.

Blue

41

RANCH COMPANIONS

Since childhood in Montana, life has taught me the true value of good dogs. Loyal, true, faithful in good or bad times, they will follow you anywhere, or stay home to guard you. They don't ask for much, just a pat on the head and a few kind words. A smart dog has incredible eye contact and communicates in silent understanding. If I am sad, my dogs are sad. When I am happy, my dogs are excited and happy. They are well-mannered and don't bark unless it is warranted. They know we are a family and treat each other kindly, including the cats or other pets I might acquire. Each evening, we have a dog party—the dogs sit in a semi-circle to see what might be a party treat. Only when their names are called do they accept their treats, never trying to take the other dog's reward. Being cattle dogs, their happiest time is helping move the herd. Swift kicks don't deter them. They just pick themselves up, shake it off and continue with their job. Three great dogs sit together on the back of my ATV as we drive around the ranch. Sadly, dogs only live for ten or so years. Some have died in the line of duty, leaving a deep void. I have often thought, a dog should live

Cody

as long as their master. However, their short life span entitles us many great dogs.

Dillon was my first New Mexico cow dog. She was purchased from a cattle ranch in Dillon, Montana. Smaller than most Australian shepherds, and solid black, she was smart and extremely athletic, making her a great dog to help gather and drive cows. After three years, I lost her to a pack of coyotes. She had been doing the work of two cowboys when she was grabbed behind the herd. I now have Ringo, a blue healer; Blue, a border collie-kelpie cross and Cody, a border collie-Australian shepherd cross. Ringo, Cody and Blue are my constant companions, working cattle together, each with his or her own style.

In Montana, my brother Bud had several cow dogs. One summer, Spot was run over by the hay mower. He disappeared into the brush, not to be found. Three years later when Buddy was bringing in cattle with his other dogs, he saw a strange object moving the cattle on the outer side of the herd. It was Spot walking on his front legs, his hind legs missing. Where had he been? How had he survived for three years and how did he make it home to once again help gather his master's cows? What a story of a great and faithful friend!

Ringo

My other companions are two cats—Happy, the Siamese and El Gato, a gray tabby, twenty-eight years old. He's the oldest cat I've ever known. El Gato loves to ride on the ATV with me. He's had several strokes this year, repeatedly recovering and today is doing well. Cats do have nine lives! My only, in-house furry friend is Roman the ferret. He's fun, funny, loving and follows me around the house, when not on the trail of a mouse.

A pigeon blew in with a storm. I named her Coo Coo. She settled in the barn, and soon became friendly, often flying to the house to find me. When I rode the ATV she followed ten feet above. The three dogs on the back of my ATV, my two sheep, Me and Ewe, running along side, a very old Grey Tabby cat in front and Coo Coo flying above were a sight to see. One day, a few miles from the house, a peregrin

Roman

falcon grabbed Coo Coo in mid-air a few feet above my ATV. Only a few
feathers remained as they slowly drifted to the earth.

Calvin Swine, my black and white Pot-Bellied pig was born in Tucson
before I moved to New Mexico. Truly a designer pig, wearing his cowboy
hat, holster and gun, he went on most of my ambulatory calls with me. He
opened the sliding glass door with his nose, coming and going in and out
of the house as he pleased. Always clean, Calvin never created a mess in
the house. Dancing, sitting and singing on command, he was a source of
entertainment and could not be left behind. He ate like a pig. After moving
to New Mexico, he gained two hundred pounds. His fat fell over his eyes,
blinding him. Adjusting to this handicap, he did well at the ranch. Because
his legs were so short, he had to put it in four-wheel drive to make it through
the mud. Living sixteen years, he by-passed his expected life span by ten
years. He too was a special friend, now missed!

Calvin Swine

42

PREDATORS

Respecting and admiring all animals causes me to have emotional conflict about predatory animals so numerous on this ranch. While in Washington, I raised three orphaned coyotes. At obedience school, they proved their intelligence and, at home, were trustworthy pets. I was veterinarian for several domesticated wolves. They were better mannered than most of my other canine patients. Now I have lost two good cow dogs to coyote packs, Dillon and later Jake, snatched while helping me drive cattle. Blue and her mother were both attacked by wolves in the front yard, in the middle of the day. A rifle shot into the air saved these two dogs.

The Mexican wolf is considered an endangered species and is being reintroduced into New Mexico. Biologists feed these wolves before their release, therefore, they have little fear of people. They have stalked school children in my county, so the school district built cages for the children to stay in until their rides home arrive. Reintroducing the wolf here comes at a price to taxpayers at more than $400,000 per wolf. It is estimated the wolves will kill more than 7,000 head of livestock and wild game over the next five years, and the financial loss to the Southwest will exceed sixty-million dollars.

The wolves I have seen don't seem intimidated by my presence. As a child in Montana, I remember pictures of dead wolves proudly displayed by trappers and hunters. These photos always made me sad. In some northern states, the number of reintroduced wolves, has grown and they are off the endangered list to be hunted again, to suffer the same demise as the wolves killed many years ago. When the New Mexico wolves are no longer endangered, they will face the same demise. In the meantime, during their reintroduction, they suffer from fright during their capture and, in many cases, recapture, collaring and transporting. Non-pure wolf litters are hunted down and killed by the federal government. Wolves are not bad. Why should they be reintroduced to again suffer at the hand of man and to cause suffering and destruction of livestock and wild game? Where is the common sense and humanity of man who claims to be the defender of wildlife?

I have had two confirmed losses from mountain lions. Deciding to raise a foal in New Mexico, I purchased the last daughter of Hai Karatie. She had a beautiful bay filly. After working with her for two months, I turned her out with her mother. They ran up a hill, a short distance from the house. A few minutes later, the mare ran back to the corral, covered in deep claw marks. The foal lay dead and mutilated. My two pet sheep, named Me and Ewe, lived under the elevated barn, near the house. They would graze nearby. They were gentle and fun, often following behind my ATV. One evening, Me came racing home without Ewe. Following his tracks, I found Ewe partially buried under a pile of leaves, her body revealing deep claw marks, her wool scattered. Me was so distraught that he hid under the barn and cried for days. Early the next morning the lion returned to the kill site. He was run up a tree by the dogs and killed with one shot. How many calves have been killed by the lions, will never be known. Bawling, heavily "bagged up" cows signal that some predator has taken a calf. Their range is too large to be frequently monitored.

Although, I earned a gold medal in rifle club, I am not a hunter. For protection, I often carry a gun while riding. A higher power has reasons for the predators. I was put on this earth to save animals, and thus have difficultly with their deaths, whatever the cause.

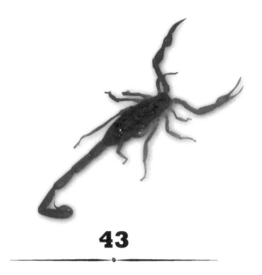

43

SNAKES, SCORPIONS AND RATS

King snakes are a welcome sight, as they kill rattlesnakes and the rats that frequent my home. Some summers I see no rattle-snakes, some summers they seem to be everywhere. One summer, they were determined to take up residency at my house. Six, including a rare western black rattler, were found under my clothesline within a week. Ringo warned me, possibly saving me from a fatal strike. My dogs, by nature, do not approach snakes. They bark and stay their distance. Having treated numerous animals in Arizona for snakebite, I know how lethal they can be. A guest, showering in the bunkhouse, left the door open and a rattler crawled in behind him. The six-foot snake curled up on the floor just outside the shower stall. Emerging with towel in hand, my guest almost stepped on it. As the diamondback struck, he snapped it with his towel, breaking the aim of the strike. The snake retreated under my guest's bed.

I was unaware of the toxicity of scorpions when I first moved to the ranch, as Arizona scorpions caused me no problem. Leaving my shirt on the floor gave me a painful awareness. While putting it on, I received four scorpion stings on my back. Their venom was so toxic that I became nauseous and suffered nerve paralysis. I have twice gone to the hospital for an EKG after the pain of a scorpion bite on my left hand traveled up my arm and down into my chest causing heart palpitations. Interestingly, I've found that, after about two weeks, the pain recedes back up the path it traveled and out through the scorpion's injection point. According to poison control, scorpion stings are not dangerous unless they are bark scorpions found in Southwest New Mexico. My type of scorpions! Before going to bed, I now search the house with a black light that turns scorpions a bright green. These I kill. Roman, the ferret, joins me on my nightly hunt.

Rats are prevalent and determined to live in my home. If they are poisoned they die in the walls and the odor forces me to stay outside. They usually outsmart traps. Saddles must be hung from the ceiling not placed on saddle racks. Food is kept in sealed containers.

I guess I will never win the battle, so my life goes on with the brown furry guests.

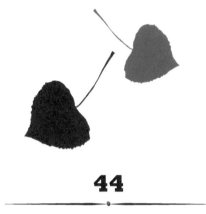

44

HEAVEN GAINS TWO MORE ANGELS

Calling from Tucson, Wendy told me Sheila's health had deteriorated. "Sheila is dying," she said. "She wants you to come to her dying party." A dying party, no one else would arrange a dying party. Dressed in black and wearing a huge Mexican wooden cross, I drove to Tucson. Sheila had become a major part of my life. I would greatly miss her. Driving through the thick mesquite forest, past her pink stalls, I parked in front of the old pink stucco house she had built. She had never allowed me into her home before. A nurse met me outside and escorted me down the old dirty hall lined with books. "Through that door," she said. "She's expecting you." Opening the door, I saw Sheila slumped down in the old mattress, looking small and frail, but she had combed her hair and wore red lipstick. Her Derringer at her side, her face lit up with a big smile. From behind the door walked effervescent Wendy. "Surprise!" they both yelled. "Happy Birthday, Doc!" I had not given a thought to my birthday, but these two special friends had. They presented me with a birthday cake, decorated with an image of Karatie. How very special was this? Sheila and Wendy beamed in delight. A dinner of crab legs had been catered and I was presented with a bottle of Sheila's favorite whiskey, Yukon Jack. Three special friends consumed the bottle of whiskey and told wild stories late into the night.

Soon Sheila did pass on, out from the mesquite thicket, through the monsoon clouds, into heaven. She's probably the only angel packing a Derringer. Her service was at Tucson's great St. Augustine Cathedral and the Bishop spoke to a packed house. Later, Wendy and I were to bury Sheila's ashes. Every shovel of dirt revealed bones of some animal she'd buried over the last fifty years. She should be set free in the mesquites, we decided, casting her ashes to the wind. The Mesquite trees bent as lightning cracked, just like the day I met her. Sheila and her Derringer would always be fondly remembered.

Soon after Sheila passed on, my mother died at the age of ninety-six. She had outlived three husbands. Until her last day, she looked like a small

My mother at 90 years old

Hai Karatie babysits my grandaughter, Heather.

porcelain doll. Hallie splendidly saw that her grandmother was well treated in her Seattle nursing home. Having always loved the Pacific Ocean, her ashes were set to the sea as white doves were released from the boat. Another angel had gone home.

Karatie, now thirty-six is still sorting cattle and babysitting grandkids. He had never been sick or lame in his life. Always the athlete, always the friend and always dependable, his shiny black bay coat has now turned gray around his beautiful gentle eyes and his soft muzzle. Walking up the road this morning, he suddenly stumbled and fell. As I rested his head in my lap his nostrils fluttered as he took his last breath and drifted from my world.

God has given me many extra special horses: Flicka, Mike, Blossom, Hitan and Hai Karatie[+]. Karatie has left me with the biggest void. He gave me pleasure and strength for thirty-six years. I miss him and wonder how I can run this ranch with out him? God has taken my best friend home.

45

ENVIRONMENTAL AWARENESS

Mother spent hours trying to instill some etiquette in me. Hours of walking with a book on my head to insure good posture were now thrown to the wind. My ranch survival demanded constant observation of the ground I walked upon, always on the lookout for scorpions, rattlesnakes and animal tracks. I have become a good tracker, knowing when and from what direction tracks were made. I also am keenly aware of predators' eating habits. Scat with hair and blood indicate a recent kill; scat with juniper berries, mesquite beans and other vegetable matter indicate a predator on a vegetarian diet, at least for the time being. Tracks around the dirt water tanks often tell a story. Careful observation might reveal deer tracks, followed by wolf or coyote tracks, then by bear or lion tracks. Circling buzzards usually indicate a kill. During the winter, the migrating bald eagles often join the buzzards, crows and ravens feasting on a dead cow. Nature has its own garbage disposal system. Grazing cows often obtain their calcium and phosphorus by eating the white bleached bones of dead cows. Bear hair is seen hanging on barbs of wire fences. Lions are seldom seen, as they are nocturnal. Their presence is usually found after a kill. Burying their prey under leaves and dirt, they nearly always return early the next day to finish consuming their prey. I live in a world where I am constantly reminded that my life revolves around survival of the fittest.

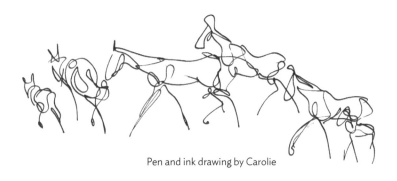

Pen and ink drawing by Carolie

46

FIRE STORM

It's been nine months and the drought continues. The hoped-for monsoon rains have not come north out of Mexico. These rains are the salvation of the Southwest. From Texas to California, the worst drought in 120 years persists in the year of 2011. I can only pray for a storm!

The storm has arrived, not with rain, but with fire! Surrounded by forest fires on three sides, the largest fire is burning fifteen miles northwest of me. As of today, it has burned more than 500,000 acres and communities in Arizona. It is only two miles from a town in New Mexico. More than 3,000 firefighters are employed. This is the tenth day of the fire and still it rages with zero percent contained. Until now, strong winds have blown from the southwest and thus held the fire north of the ranch. The winds have stopped today; the valley is choked with smoke. The fires have pulled the oxygen from the air and the heat is nearly unbearable. Visibility is less than a mile. The air reminds me of bitter cold Montana days when ice crystals hung in the air. The Montana natives called it "cold smoke." I spent the morning traveling forty miles over rough, rocky terrain to try to evaluate the fire's progress, but thick smoke prevented my surveillance. The ranch's western border is the fence line between New Mexico and Arizona. The Arizona side contains the "Blue," a heavily timbered primitive area. If a northwest wind blows, the Blue would be a tinder-box for the raging fire that could spill over onto my ranch.

To the south is another large wild fire in Arizona's Chiricahua Mountains near the Mexican border. As the Mexican border is a hundred miles south of me, the fire is not a threat, but its smoke has come north and hangs heavy in the air. A few miles east of me, the Gila Wilderness Fire has been burning for an entire month and is only fifty-percent contained. It has burned more than 150,000 acres. With no wind today, its smoke has joined with smoke of the other two fires. My beautiful mountain view has been reduced to a gray and eerie shroud that burns my eyes and lungs. I saw only a few cattle this morning through the smoke. They appeared as dark ghost-like shadows drifting through the timber. The cows I saw yesterday were nowhere to be seen today. If the fire comes here, I wonder if I could move the drought-stricken, weakened cattle down the mountain to safety?

The cattle have grazed away even the mesquite near the spring. As this is the only water source for miles, the fire has pushed the elk, deer, javalina, lions, and all other forms of wildlife to water here. I see numerous bear tracks and bear hair on the fence. A large tiger-striped cow lay dead near the spring. Twenty yards away, lay another dead cow. A call to the New Mexico Game and Fish resulted in their setting a snare trap near one dead cow. They tell me once a bear kills cattle, it is likely to continue to do so and this bear will be snared and shot, not transported to another area. A few hours later the snare had been sprung, but the bear got away. Just before dark, my friend Ray and I returned to the spring. The bear was returning to the dead cow. One shot through its heart and it was dead.

Desperate for stock water away from the spring and all the bears, Ray and I repaired a galvanized pipeline running two miles up the mountain, from a spring in a far north canyon, to a 50,000-gallon metal rim tank. The galvanized two-inch pipe-line had not been used in fifty years. It was full of dead mice and their nesting material. After two weeks of hiking up and down the rocky mountain to repair the broken and plugged line, the pipe was free of mice and ready to go. Ray had the patience of Job during this challenge. Known for his mechanical skills, he made, from many spare parts, the mighty little ejection pump. He talked to it like I talk to my animals. He made it purr as he convinced it to move the water one thousand feet in elevation up the mountain to the rim tank. The water then, by way of gravity, flowed water to three drinkers. The spring and this rim tank are now the only water source for the cattle, as the dirt tanks have been dry for months. After turning the valves to fill these drinkers, as I wait, I sit under a juniper tree and visit with my three faithful dogs.

Memories of this rim tank return from four years ago, when the mountain behind me had a raging forest fire. The district ranger called and asked if firefighters could use my tank water on the fire. "Sure," I said. I'd been moving cattle that hot summer day and that rim tank had become my swimming hole. Forgetting about the Forest Service request, I tied my horse to a tree, shed my sweaty clothes and climbed into the refreshing water. A short time later, I saw a helicopter, with a large swinging water bucket heading for the tank. I tried to hide, but couldn't. Frantically, I waved my arms. The pilot finally saw me and buzzed off. Imagine what some hot, tired firefighter would think if a nude woman had fallen out of the sky, onto their fire line!

47

BEARS AND MORE BEARS

Resting in the shade of the rim tank and reminiscing about this incident, I had the feeling that something was watching me. The dogs were alerted. A bear was nearby in the brush. We loaded up on the ATV, my three dogs sitting in the back. We were five miles from home and had not seen one cow. Usually, a hundred or more cows came for water that time of day. Were the bears now running the cows out of their only other water source, the rim tank? I saw what appeared to be a dark-colored cow running toward us. It was a huge bear! I thought it would stop and run away when it heard the ATV. Instead, it ran faster in my direction! When it got thirty feet away, the dogs began to bark. The bear reared up on its hind legs, then barreled toward us at full speed. I pushed on the throttle, passing it just before it reached us on the road. The next morning I saw a large sow with two tiny cubs. Was this the bear that chased me, as she likely had left her cubs on the other side of the road? There were bears everywhere! They had now run the cows from both the rim tank and the spring. The cows and calves now had no safe place to drink. The evening news reported a woman walking her dog had been attacked and killed by a bear. There are no grizzly bear in New Mexico, but the hungry black bear were abnormally dangerous because of the fires and drought.

My friend and I again went to the spring where he had shot the bear that killed the first two cows. We found many bear tracks and the stench of death hung in the air. Turkey vultures with their naked red heads filled the sky in the giant cottonwood trees. Suddenly, two bears ran for the timber at the same time. They vanished before we could fire off a shot. The next morning we found eight more dead cows and one dead calf. I knew I had branded the little black steer three months earlier as its ear tag lay beside it on the ground. A bear had grabbed the calf and then its protective red mother, dragging her down the mountain, leaving a long drag mark. Many nervous "bagged up" cows bawled for their calves. I estimated forty calves and twelve mother cows to be lost to the bears. Again, I prayed for rain.

Ray, bear hunting at the spring

48

THOR, THE THUNDER GOD

Gray and white clouds billowed above the four mountain ranges that surround the ranch. Blue sky intermittently danced between them as they rose higher and higher. Was this a mirage? After nine months without rain, could this possibly be the beginning of the monsoon? There had been a few sightings of virga, the streaks of rain that never reach the hot dry ground. But now, these clouds were growing heavy and the blue sky was being replaced. A distant rumble broke the still silence of the hot, humid day. The stillness ended abruptly with a swirling wind blowing dust and leaves across the parched land. I could smell rain! Would it possibly reach the ground?

Standing in the corral I yelled, "Come on down!" I did the best rain dance I knew and shouted my invitation again. Wind swirled around me. I knew my guardian angel was dancing with me. We did the two-step and the Montana stomp. My guardian angel had worked overtime this year, but he didn't leave me. He laced me with resilience and pulled me up by my belt loops whenever I thought of giving up in despair. As we danced around the

Tracking the Herd

old wooden corral, the sound of rifles cracked through the air and bounced off the mountains. Lightning danced vertically and horizontally. Thor the Thunder God had made a strike! The heavens parted and the rain came down! It came hard and it came fast. It was as though the Big Dipper had spilled all the water in its ladle. My prayers had been answered. It was now possible to save the cattle and the ranch!

There was no water runoff from this rain, as the thirsty earth devoured every raindrop. It would have to rain like this again to reach the grass roots and to fill the forty-three dirt tanks that had been dry for months, but this was a start. The whole range was charged with new energy, as was I. The cattle and horses were on the move. As the rain diminished and the sun reappeared, birds began to sing. Frogs emerged from the soil and croaked throughout the day and night. Life had been reborn and I knew the sky held a promise that more rain was on the way.

I rode my horse to the spring and to the rim tank to see if the bears had killed more cattle. There were no cattle to be found. They had all moved out, but where did they go? They had left all the water to avoid the bears. A search for their tracks led me ten miles up a steep trail to a high mountain pasture with no water.

There was not a cloud in the sky, and no rain was predicted. I couldn't leave them without water. Having no choice, I gathered the cattle for eight hours, driving them down the other side of the mountain, to a nine-hundred foot well. I then drove my stock trailer back up the mountain to retrieve my four horses. As I topped the ridge, I could only see three of them. Clouds were forming. I loaded the three horses and waited for the fourth to show up. Within seconds, a most unexpected and dramatic storm occurred. Lightning cracked as the rain came down in torrents. The road filled with water and I could not see out the windows. The horses rocked the stock trailer in fright. Thirty minutes later, the rain let up a bit. I heard a whinny from Sun Dance as he ran over the hill, looking for the other three horses. They whinnied back and he came running. Sun Dance stood, shaking, behind the trailer. It was still raining hard. It would be a miracle if I could load him in that storm. With only a piece of bailing twine to catch him, I slipped it around his neck. He was more than willing to load. Just as I closed the trailer gate, a bolt of lightning hit so close I thought it had hit the trailer. Thor was back! I was shaking, the horses were shaking, and the dogs were shaking. The storm resumed its intensity! With the wipers on, I still could not see out the window for another hour. Finally, the rain slowed and I began my thousand-foot drop down the road with the horses. Everything on the truck that could be geared down was on low and slow, as the trailer brakes weren't working. The top of the road was graveled. The deep canyon to the south was a constant threat. Suddenly, the gravel turned to slick red clay. The trailer pushed the truck sideways, toward the canyon edge! Without brakes, I dropped the trailer wheels into the ditch on the upside of the road. If the truck went off into the canyon, all of us would be killed. The storm again intensified. My only chance was to unload the frightened horses. The red clay was slick as grease. I fell before reaching the back of the trailer. The horses were reluctant to jump onto the steep, slick surface, but being good ranch horses, I unloaded them without getting crushed. Having lightened my load by four thousand pounds, I again tried to drive to the bottom. Each try took me closer to the canyon edge. I resigned to the possibility that I would spend the night in the truck. It was not cold, but I was soaking wet, tired and hungry. I knew no one would be coming up the road. After two more hours, the rain slowed. Water no longer ran down the road. One more effort, as it was getting dark! My dogs were my moral support. I inched forward, finally guiding the front truck wheel into the uphill ditch I slowly drove home.

The old saying in the west—"If you don't like the weather, wait it will change"—was never so true. I had waited nearly a year. The rain that had me dancing in the corral was just a sneak preview to this storm. The scary moments were outweighed by the knowledge that, in all its violence, this storm filled the earth cracked dirt tanks, watered the grass to the roots and rejuvenated the parched land. How did the cattle and horses know this storm was coming? Somehow they knew! They had left the spring and the bears, trailed ten miles up a steep mountain, and waited there for two days without water. The miracles of nature are incredible. Now, after one week of grass and water, the cattle are recovering in weight and strength. Several have had new calves. My symbol of survival, Peek A Boo, my beautiful gray Brahma steer, now eleven years old, and seventeen hands tall with three foot horns is following me across the pasture We made it! We survived the worst drought in 120 years, the largest forest fires in New Mexico and Arizona history, and the starving bears.

49

SATURDAY NIGHT

A ll work and no play. Not me! Saturday night at the Blue Front Bar and Café in Glenwood for dining and dancing are necessary for my survival. Living alone like a hermit on this mountain can be tolerated only so long. It's called cabin fever and, like any fever, needs a cure. A good western band, and a few drinks are medical miracles. Bucky, the café owner, cook, singer and guitar player gathers up his group of talented musicians and the cares of the week disappear as the music rolls on. Western dances in small western towns are extraordinary. Dancers pack the floor by the middle of the first song. From ranching couples in their golden years to young buckaroos, the dance becomes vibrant. Though the area is small in population, people seem to come out of nowhere, happy to greet their friends. If a stranger appears, the locals are quick to make them feel welcome. Cuddling up and dancing under the shadow of a cowboy's Stetson is still the closest thing to heaven!

Entrance to Rocking Arrow Ranch

50

GOING FULL CIRCLE

My life has been filled with many chapters, mostly good ones. Without valleys, there would be no mountains. I have climbed a lot of peaks and often dropped back down into the valleys. These low spots have been a spring-board for learning from my mistakes and creating my resilience. A sense of humor is necessary for survival, as sometimes life seems to make no sense. My motto—"work hard, play hard"—is still in full force.

Being a World War II baby, my body is not as young as my heart. Friends call me the Bionic Woman, as most of my body parts have been re-arranged or replaced with titanium. My medical history reads like a head to toe makeover: multiple fractures of the jaw; fusion of my neck with bone from my pelvis; three compression fractures of the thoracic vertebrae; fusion and titanium plating of the lumbar vertebrae; two shoulder surgeries, fingers replaced with tendons from my foot, two hip replacements, two knee surgeries, and joints of both feet replaced by titanium.

Metabolically, I am perfect. All internal organs are functioning at top performance. My heart is big and strong. My brain sometimes tells my body to do crazy things, but otherwise seems to function normally. My shoulder and back injuries prevent me from heavy lifting, but I still build fence, ride my horse from daylight to dark, sort and brand cattle and can dance all night. My western artwork is always a challenge and provides peaceful quiet time. Nature's ever-changing beauty surrounds me. I have left footsteps in the snow, the sand, and the mud. Heaven, I'm sure, is beautiful, but I have been blessed, for the time, with heaven on earth. Having gone full circle, I am again enveloped under a blue sky, in the cradle of the Rocky Mountains.

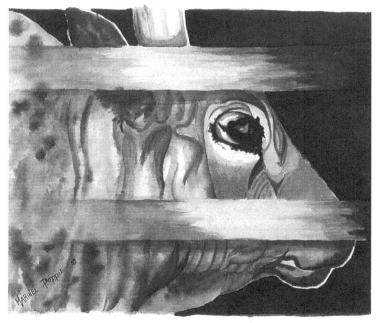

Peek-A-Boo, my symbol of survival.

ABOUT THE AUTHOR

Marinel J. Poppie was raised in Montana where she was active in high school and college rodeo and ski teams. She attended Colorado, Montana and Washington Universities receiving her doctorate in Veterinary Medicine and has been an active equine veterinarian for 46 years. She has trained and shown nearly every type of horse including reining, stock horses, hunters and jumpers, and gaited horses, rodeo trick horses and completed several 100 mile endurances races. Fascinated by the beauty of Montana and the Southwest she is very involved in the daily tasks of the working rancher. Her artwork of watercolors, oils and bronze are exhibited and sold in Montana, Arizona, and New Mexico. She is presently owner and manager of the Rocking Arrow Cattle Company near Glenwood, New Mexico.

Made in United States
Troutdale, OR
06/16/2024

20596771R00130